W9-DEO-171

NO. 5, FALL 1997

NEW DIRECTIONS FOR SCHOOL LEADERSHIP

On

Being a

Principal

The Rewards
and Challenges
of School Leadership

RICHARD H. ACKERMAN
University of Massachusetts Lowell
Harvard Graduate School of Education
EDITOR-IN-CHIEF

GORDON A. DONALDSON JR.
University of Maine
EDITOR

ON BEING A PRINCIPAL: THE REWARDS AND CHALLENGES OF
SCHOOL LEADERSHIP
Gordon A. Donaldson Jr. (ed.)
New Directions for School Leadership, No. 5, Fall 1997
Richard H. Ackerman, Editor-in-Chief

© 1997 by Jossey-Bass Inc., Publishers.

Microfilm copies of issues and articles are available in 16 mm and 35 mm, as well as
microfiche in 105 mm, through University Microfilms Inc., 300 North Zeeb Road,
Ann Arbor, Michigan 48106-1346.

ISSN 1089-5612   ISBN 0-7879-9856-7

NEW DIRECTIONS FOR SCHOOL LEADERSHIP is part of The Jossey-Bass Education
Series and is published quarterly by Jossey-Bass Inc., Publishers, 350 Sansome Street,
San Francisco, California 94104-1342.

SUBSCRIPTIONS: Please see Ordering Information on p. iv.
EDITORIAL CORRESPONDENCE should be sent to Richard Ackerman, The Principals'
Center, Harvard Graduate School of Education, 336 Gutman Library, Cambridge,
MA, 02138.

Jossey-Bass Web address: http://www.josseybass.com

Printed in the United States of America on acid-free recycled paper containing
100 percent recovered waste paper, of which at least 20 percent is postconsumer waste.

The International Network of Principals' Centers

The International Network of Principals' Centers sponsors *New Directions for School Leadership* as part of its commitment to strengthening leadership at the individual school level through professional development for leaders. The Network has a membership of principals' centers, academics, and practitioners in the United States and overseas and is open to all groups and institutions committed to the growth of school leaders and the improvement of schools. The Network currently functions primarily as an information exchange and support system for member centers in their efforts to work directly with school leaders in their communities. Its office is in the Principals' Center at the Harvard Graduate School of Education.

The Network offers these services:

- The International Directory of Principals' Centers features member centers with contact persons, descriptions of center activities, program references, and evaluation instruments.
- The Annual Conversation takes place every spring, when members meet for seminars, workshops, speakers, and to initiate discussions that will continue throughout the year.
- *Newsnotes*, the Network's quarterly newsletter, informs members of programs, conferences, workshops, and special interest items.
- *Reflections*, an annual journal, includes articles by principals, staff developers, university educators, and principals' center staff members.

For further information, please contact:

International Network of Principals' Centers
Harvard Graduate School of Education
336 Gutman Library
Cambridge, MA 02138
(617) 495-9812

Ordering Information

NEW DIRECTIONS FOR SCHOOL LEADERSHIP
This series of paperback books provides principals, superintendents, teachers, and others who exercise leadership at the local level with insight and guidance on the important issues influencing schools and school leadership. Books in the series are published quarterly in Fall, Winter, Spring and Summer and are available for purchase both by subscription and individually.

SUBSCRIPTIONS cost $52.00 for individuals (a savings of 35 percent over single-copy prices) and $105.00 for libraries. Prices subject to change. There are no shipping and handling charges on subscriptions.

SINGLE COPIES cost $25.00 plus shipping. There will be handling charges on billed orders. Call the 800 number below for more information.

SINGLE COPIES AVAILABLE FOR SALE
SL1   Every Teacher as a Leader: Realizing the Potential of Teacher Leadership, *Gayle Moller, Marilyn Katzenmeyer*
SL2   Boundary Crossings: Educational Partnerships and School Leadership, *Paula A. Cordeiro*
SL3   Schools for Everyone: A New Perspective on Inclusion, *Elizabeth A. Herbert*
SL4   Students Taking the Lead: The Challenges and Rewards of Empowering Youth in Schools, *Judith A. Boccia*
SL5   On Being a Principal: The Rewards and Challenges of School Leadership, *Gordon A. Donaldson Jr.*

QUANTITY DISCOUNTS ARE AVAILABLE. Please contact Jossey-Bass Periodicals for information at 1-415-433-1740.

TO ORDER, CALL 1-800-956-7739 or 1-415-433-1767
. . . and visit our website at http://www.josseybass.com

Contents

Just what are the rewards of school leadership? This preview of On Being a Principal: The Rewards and Challenges of School Leadership *highlights central themes in the authors' responses to this question.*

1

Seeing the possibilities

Gordon A. Donaldson Jr.

IN A TIME when principals are, as Ernest Boyer once wrote of high schools, "accumulating purposes like barnacles on a weathered ship," principals themselves find it increasingly difficult to know their function in the school (1981, p. 57). We are all familiar with the problems attendant upon this condition: The school's constituencies (including the staff) enjoy "open season" on principals; respected educators find the principalship unattractive and either leave it or avoid it; schools flounder in a morass of conflicting conceptions of how their leaders should function. It is not a pretty picture.

This, the fifth volume of *New Directions for School Leadership*, explores what makes the principalship worth doing. We have invited principals to write about what is rewarding to them about the work they do. Their words are poignant and revelatory. Writing in the spring of 1997, most of our authors struggled to make time and energy simply to reflect on the question, What is rewarding to me about this work? Their stories reveal just how immediate and human the rewards are: an interchange with a child or the sudden realization that a long-sought-after change has indeed taken

NEW DIRECTIONS FOR SCHOOL LEADERSHIP, NO. 5, FALL 1997 © JOSSEY-BASS PUBLISHERS

root. They also reveal just how subtly principals discover that they are making a difference.

Why have we devoted an issue of *New Directions for School Leadership* to this topic? It is remarkable how little we know about what keeps good principals going. As the going gets tougher for school leaders and as we see wonderful teachers increasingly choosing not to become principals, the need to learn more about what is rewarding in school leadership work becomes more urgent. In his marvelous work *The Call of Service: A Witness to Idealism* (1993), Robert Coles explores this question among volunteers, social and political activists, and charity workers. From interviews, he gleans some hazards of this work that are familiar to principals: weariness, cynicism, anger, despair, and burnout. He also elicits the satisfactions: achieving a goal, serving a moral purpose, experiencing personal affirmation, enduring when the odds are against you, establishing a career. Reading *The Call to Service* leaves me buoyed and hopeful yet sharply aware of the hazards of service work. This edition of *New Directions for School Leadership*, in its autobiographical explorations of the satisfactions of school leadership, is intended to affect its readers in a similar fashion.

In my interchanges with the authors during the preparation of this issue, I learned three things about the nature of school leadership rewards. Most of these principals identified first their schools' accomplishments. They wrote of the new block schedule, the grandparent volunteer program, the citation from the state, the successful transition to magnet school status, or the achievement of a more positive climate in the halls of the school. Indeed, these accomplishments are grand ones. Such changes represent the culmination of hard leadership work, work that presumably paid off in better services for children. Any principal who can point to an accomplishment of this sort has reason to celebrate!

But, as the reader will see, these school-level achievements were not the most personally rewarding for most authors. I cannot say precisely why. My educated guess is that such achievements are somewhat depersonalized and distant from what principals do every day. Perhaps the credit for them more properly belongs with teachers, parents, and kids. Perhaps they are hard to relate to the myriad of activities and personal contacts that make up the leader's daily work. The real work of these principals is not only in the long-term institutional changes they and their staffs seek, it is more so in the personal dilemmas presented by children and parents and the professional challenges presented by staff. Here, beyond the rewards of institutional growth, lies a second type of reward, a satisfaction arising more immediately from working with the people of the school.

Our writers dwell much longer and in more detail on these rewards than they do on the first type. They share vignettes depicting how they enjoyed helping Julie resolve her reading quandary or helping Pat's mother come to a new understanding of what the school can do for Pat given his special needs, and they write of the collaboration they have helped develop within their staffs and of including students in problem solving and leadership for the school. It is clear from these stories that good principals are sustained by seeing their efforts pay off in the evidence of their daily work with children, families, and staff, one child or one teacher at a time. These rewards remind me of Ronald Heifetz' observation that "leadership takes place every day. It is neither the traits of the few, a rare event, or a once-in-a-lifetime opportunity" (1994, p. 275).

Beyond these two types of rewards—seeing institutional accomplishments and being of service to people—lies a third type. This type is the most intriguing to me because it seems to stem more from the personal than from the professional experience of being a principal. It is not so much derived from *what the principal makes happen* as it is from the very experience of being an active, hands-on leader in a school community. Most of our authors derived immense satisfaction from being enmeshed in the action of something as important as growing minds, bodies, and psyches. For many, the constant variety and human contact of this work pressed them to keep learning, to flex, to be stimulated and alive.

Our writers enjoy their contacts with people and seem to draw sustenance from the humor, the tears, the incongruities, the open emotion, the sheer life of the school. We can feel Phil Hunsberger's fondness for his students and the poignancy of Suzanne Olson's relationship with Jo. We sense it in the amusement Gordon Nunemaker harvests from his daily experience and in Paul Bianchi's wit. Participating in the lives of children, our principals treasure their place and seem affirmed by the immediacy of their potential to affect the lives of others while they celebrate the effects of the children's lives on their own.

Ultimately, this third type of reward seems to be a reminder to these writers of their humanity and of their inability single-handedly to achieve superhuman leadership feats. To a person, they write of what they have learned from children, from parents, from staff. They relate self-deprecating stories where they—along with kids and staff sometimes—laugh at themselves, as if to confirm their foibles. They write of what Barney Hallowell calls his "self-doubts" and of the importance of balancing their ambition and type A activities with contemplation, letting their hair down in fellowship with colleagues, or simply being with kids. Walter McClennen expresses the importance of keeping perspective, what Ronald Heifetz calls "getting on the balcony" to understand and appreciate better the "dance" you're in (1994; p. 252).

The act of writing has pushed our authors to "get on the balcony." Although it proved difficult for most to get to the writing task, once there they found that from the balcony they could realize not only what was frustrating to them in their work but what was rewarding. Writing to the readers of *New Directions for School Leadership* gave them an audience of colleagues with whom to share what is valuable about their work. Publishing their reflections from their balconies connects these principals with our professional community. I hope each author has found the act of writing for our community rewarding in and of itself.

Our writers have taught me that to sustain effort and hope in their own work they need to see evidence of their effects in terms of institutional growth, interpersonal success, and personal fulfillment. But they also need to feel appreciative of their work and the many partners they have in it. For this to happen, they need to know that they are appreciated, accepted for who they are, and respected for the leadership they are trying to provide. Affirmation that they belong as principals of their schools is central to each. And feeling that affirmation is often reward enough.

References

Boyer, E. *High School*. New York: Harper and Row, 1981.

Coles, R. *The Call of Service: A Witness to Idealism*. Boston: Houghton Mifflin, 1993.

Heifetz, R. A. *Leadership Without Easy Answers*. Cambridge, Mass.: Belknap Press, 1994.

GORDON A. DONALDSON JR. *is professor of education and coordinator of the Maine Network of School Leaders at the University of Maine.*

A middle school principal finds that her fulfillment as a principal grows from staying true to her values as a teacher.

2

My inspirations

Suzanne Olson

I NEVER ASPIRED to be an administrator. From the time I was six I wanted to be a teacher. I set up my first school at our backyard picnic table the summer before I entered public school. My younger brother, a most reluctant student, and some other neighborhood children served as my pupils. I was in total control of my class, my curriculum, and the length of the school day. Those were glorious days! After graduating from college, I began my teaching career in earnest. For fifteen years I taught different classes in Massachusetts and in Maine. Throughout this time, I loved what I did and could not imagine doing anything else. The challenges were great, but the successes were even greater. I grew personally and professionally from the daily direct feedback I received from the young adolescents I taught. My goal was to teach until I dropped.

In the late 1980s, the Maine Commissioner of Education invited me to serve for a year as an Instructional Support Group consultant, working with educators around the state on issues relating to the education of gifted and talented students. At the completion of the year, my school board and superintendent announced that I would return to the district as an administrator rather than as a teacher. Since that time, I have served as a central office administrator and as the building administrator for Hall-Dale Middle

NEW DIRECTIONS FOR SCHOOL LEADERSHIP, NO. 5, FALL 1997 © JOSSEY-BASS PUBLISHERS

School. In my heart, I am still a teacher who yearns for the instant, positive feedback that I once received daily from my students, but I understand that, at this moment, I have a different professional calling.

School administration has challenged me to the core of my existence. Families are more dysfunctional, time demands are greater, and resources are more limited than at any time in my twenty-five-year career. Most days I feel that the educators in our school are like elastic bands stretched to their greatest limits. Yet something internal awakens me each morning with the energy and confidence to continue the journey that left me exhausted the day before. When I reflect on what inspires me to carry on, I find myself focusing on watershed events in my five years as a building administrator. I would like to share some of these with you.

Jo

Jo was a handsome, angry sixth-grader when he arrived at our school. His father had left his mother and him when Jo was too young to remember and had played no role in Jo's life until he returned to Maine when Jo was entering middle school. Jo had learning and behavioral problems; he also knew that his young mother was dying of breast cancer. As is typical of angry twelve-year-olds, Jo spent a great deal of time in my office. During this time, I came to understand not only that I had to be consistent and fair with discipline, but also that I would have to take the time to develop an understanding of what lay beyond the anger and the aggressive behavior if I was going to impact Jo's life positively.

What began as my lesson for Jo soon became Jo's lesson for me. I came to know and feel the pain of abandonment, which both Jo and his mother felt. I also came to admire her strength, her love for her child, and her courage. Jo was at a crossroad in his life and wondered what was to become of him after his mother's death. On one hand, he wanted to stand by her, rejecting his father. On the other, he knew that he would have to face the inevitable and that moving toward his father before his mother's death might spare him some pain later. A fierce legal custody battle followed. During these months of lawyers and hearings, Jo continued to struggle with his choices and I began to understand the complexities of life that children carry with them to school on a daily basis.

As Jo's mother became sicker, she also became more reflective. Over time she came to understand that the greatest legacy she could leave her child was the ability to forgive. During her last days of life, she made peace with Jo's father and agreed that the next phase of Jo's childhood would be with his dad. She died the summer before Jo entered high school. When I attended her funeral, I was struck by Jo's composure as he entered the church with his father. As I left the church at the end of the service, Jo spotted me from the far side of the churchyard. He came running through the crowd, hugged me and said, with confidence, "I'm going to be fine, Mrs. Olson. I really am."

Jo is fine, and I learned many lessons from him and his family. Of greatest importance for me as an educational leader, and as a human being, was the notion of fighting the good fight with the understanding that the victory can take many forms.

Giving life to ideas

For many years, our school system offered foreign language classes only to college-bound high school students. Eight years ago, we formed a districtwide team to research and recommend future direction for our foreign language program. The discussions and ideas generated during these years have led our district to a place we could not have dreamed of being. All children in the third through the eighth grades now participate in foreign language instruction in French, Japanese, and Spanish. Eighty percent of our high school students continue with one or more languages throughout their high school careers.

How did this happen in a small central Maine school community? Our research taught us that students need to learn second languages early in their school careers. It also taught us that students reaching adulthood at the beginning of the millennium will be living and working in a global community and will need language and cultural experiences beyond our own. In addition, studying a second language improves thinking in the first language and increases understanding of the cultural diversity within the United States. With this knowledge, we worked to educate our community about the need for language instruction and for the systematic implementation of programs in lower grades. In the fall of 1990, we moved into the middle school arena and offered French, Latin, and Spanish to all sixth- through eighth-grade students.

Two years later, we received a Critical Areas Language grant from the U.S. Department of Education. Our foreign language study group decided that this was an excellent time to move to a more inclusive foreign language program, so we added Japanese to our repertoire. With grant in hand, we then approached our school board and proposed that the local community support the study of French and Spanish in the elementary grades so that we could offer a program comparable to that in our secondary schools. Because of the community's long-term support of education and the past success of the program, the board agreed to our request.

We have not only continued beyond the grant period, but we have been able to expand the Japanese program into our high school and have two native-speaking Japanese teachers teaching grades three through eleven. What began as an interesting idea has become an integral part of the educational program of all students in our small school district. When I began the promotion of this program, I took a long, hard look at the paradigm of foreign language instruction as "frill." When I was a student in the fifties and sixties, foreign language instruction was, generally, an intellectual exercise. For adults in the new millennium, it will be essential. My passionate belief in this program for all students played a major role in its coming to fruition.

One of the benchmarks of professional success for me is whether or not a good idea has a life beyond the people who create it. I believe that this program will enrich the lives of children and the community at large well beyond my tenure in education. This will be a part of my personal legacy.

Moving beyond the unknown

On a daily basis, those of us working in education feel barraged by accusations and criticism; trust in the institution of education is not a given. It must be earned over and over again. As a staff, we have deep concern about the lack of understanding and respect for differences among people. Hate crimes impact the lives of children in small Maine communities. Long ago we learned as a staff that we could try to cover up or ignore the hateful language we overheard in the hallways, or we could admit that we had a problem and attempt to rally the community to take action. We chose, with some trepidation, the latter.

Our students and staff are actively involved with the Maine Office of the Attorney General in piloting a civil rights team in our school. The mission of this team is to serve as a clearinghouse for student and staff concerns and as educators in the area of diversity and respect. This is difficult work and we often find ourselves in conflict about the tone and pace of our highly sensitive mission. To succeed requires that both adults and students open their hearts and minds in ways they may not have before. The stakes are high; the risks are great. As adults we are venturing into an arena that is new to many of us.

Our high school drama group had recently performed "The Lottery," a play based on a Shirley Jackson short story. In the drama, the members of a rural turn-of-the-century community annually stone to death one of their members in order to ensure a good harvest of corn. A staff member, and member of the civil rights team, suggested that the drama group perform the play for our middle school students and staff. Great debate began among the faculty as to the risks involved in sponsoring such a production. Some adults worried that the message was too obscure; some feared that we would have a backlash from the parents. After discussing the pros and cons with the student members of the civil rights team, we decided we would present the play.

During the twenty-minute production, I was in personal distress. The production was wonderfully acted; everyone in the audience was absolutely quiet (no small feat for middle school students on a Friday afternoon!). My heart was racing; I felt like vomiting. My head was pounding with thoughts: Was this too risky? What if we could not generate the dialogue necessary to pull this off? Had we gone too far this time? My more optimistic self responded with, "You know the power of this group of students and staff. Trust that they will rise to the occasion."

When the performance ended, the theater was absolutely silent. The cast returned to the front of the stage and began a dialogue with the audience. For the next thirty minutes, Hall-Dale Middle School students engaged in the most profound conversation about convention, insiders and outsiders, and personal ethics in which I have ever been involved. As the students walked to their buses, they were still debating the issues. The only parental calls we received were from people who had had meaningful conversations with their children and wished they, too, had the opportunity to personally participate.

Learning, for all of us, means moving beyond the known to the unknown. Our Friday afternoon performance of "The Lottery" gave us all the confidence to take the risks necessary to effect meaningful change in American education. It also reminded us that students know what challenges they can meet; we just need to remember to ask them.

Gathering energy from within

During my years as a teacher, I had the luxury of focusing my total energy on kids. Adults were helpful only when they could contribute to my professional development and, as a result, I could do better work with kids. Once I found myself in an administrative role, there was a solid layer of teachers between me and the students. My new challenge was to motivate and support adults so that they could inspire kids. Without warning or choice, I had become the support staff for the teachers in the trenches and I was not very happy being there.

What I soon came to understand was that adult learners are like child learners. They are at different developmental levels that do not necessarily correspond with length of time in the profession. If we were going to be successful, we would have to determine what each person needed and how those needs could best be met. I also discovered that the middle school staff was quite homogeneous. Most were in their forties, had been educated in Maine, and had taught nowhere but at our school. They had come of age as educators during a time when teachers worked in isolation in their classrooms and sank or swam on their own.

What has transpired during the past four years gives me the inspiration to continue my administrative work. We have had the opportunity to hire new faculty within each teacher team. Our staff is now diverse in age, experience, and cultural background. Now I watch young faculty members move veterans' thinking in ways no administrator ever could. They can do this because they are open, eager, and nonjudgmental. They show deep respect for the repertoire of teaching and classroom management strategies the veteran staff members are willing to share with them. It is exciting for me to watch a young and energetic math teacher bond with a veteran teacher. Their professional alliance has brought great change in mathematics instruction in both schools. For many years, my school's math staff were less innovative than the staff in other departments. Now I am running to keep up, and I love the pace.

In my teacher years, I derived satisfaction from my own work. In my administrative years, I derive satisfaction from the work of others as well as my own. I feel I am a member of a progressive, professional organization that gathers its energy and expertise from within. I can either contribute to or draw from this energy and expertise at any time on any day. The whole truly feels greater than the sum of the parts.

From reflection grows optimism

As I have settled into my role as a school administrator, I have come to spend more time in reflection. The pace of each school day is hectic and leaves me exhausted. As an antidote to this condition, I have become dependent on "found moments" when I can dwell on where we have been and where we are going. Our actions need to be precise, well-researched, built on meaningful consensus, forward-moving, and student-centered. I need time and space to help me ask: How do our actions and decisions stack up against these standards?

Because of the fatigue I feel most evenings, I save my reflective time for the early morning. Because I have always been a morning person and a runner, the dawning of each new day takes me outside onto the roadways of my town. I use this time to celebrate the beginning of a new day and new opportunities. Sometimes my running conversations with myself begin with tension and frustration carried over from a fitful night of sleep. I rehearse an upcoming phone call with a parent, consider the appropriate reentry for a student who has been in trouble, or anticipate the extra stresses on economically needy kids who get teased on the school bus. Without exception, as my body relaxes and is lulled by the rhythm of movement and the quiet of the outdoors, I am able to move mentally to an optimistic level. By the time I return home, my head is clear, my courage is strong, and I am energized for the day.

After twenty-five years, my passion for teaching has not left me; I cherish my direct contact with the young adolescents in our school. I am challenged and inspired by their emerging personhood. In reflection, I find renewal and optimism for our work and I am reminded that my personal fondness and respect for each child is the essence of my longevity in education.

SUZANNE OLSON *is principal of Hall-Dale Middle School, Hallowell, Maine.*

Leading an elementary school from the bottom to the top takes faith in the people around you and a willingness to keep learning yourself.

3

Getting it right

Al Narvaez

I WAS ASSIGNED the principal of Gardendale Elementary School in December of 1978 after having served a two-and-one-half-year apprenticeship as an assistant principal at two different elementary schools. My knowledge and emerging vision of what schools should be like had been tempered by seven years as an elementary classroom teacher and four years as a district resource teacher.

I may be considered somewhat of an enigma because I have chosen to remain at one school for so long in the face of the more popular wisdom that dictates reassignment of principals every four to six years. My usual response to the furrowed brows and "oh, really's" is that I am staying until I get it right. There may be some wisdom to the notion that true reform and school improvement is an evolving, long-term process. If the principal is to be considered one of the key players in the process, then "being there" may require longer tenures than what is now common practice.

The first ten years of my evolution as a principal is a composite of learning the craft of administration, the art of leadership, and the social and political context of schools and school systems. Most important, however, is the process of developing as a person, a human being with a very unique vocation. On a personal level, I have learned to seek the silver lining in those adversities every

NEW DIRECTIONS FOR SCHOOL LEADERSHIP, NO. 5, FALL 1997 © JOSSEY-BASS PUBLISHERS

principal experiences that cause us to question our choice of professions. More often than not, those silver linings have become a positive reality for me. At the heart of this lesson lies a cornerstone of my work: see, hear, and understand the humanity of my school colleagues, their needs, and the context in which some of those needs are met. My ability to lead is compromised when I lose sight of this reality.

The past eight years at Gardendale Elementary have taught me and retaught me the importance of remembering the humanity of those we work with. They have been a period of the greatest successes and the greatest disappointments of my career. I have learned that success and disappointment go hand in hand; you cannot have one without the other. There is something to be learned from every failed effort if one is able to put the ego aside, step back, and objectively ask, How can I get it right next time? In fact, when I ask myself, Why did this work well? I can see that the success is often tied to a prior disappointment. The satisfactions I gain from my work are not negated by my failures; they are enhanced by them!

My great disappointments occur when others, for a variety of reasons, seem to impede the path toward accomplishing goals. Often external forces such as state and district mandates and procedures, union contracts, and uninformed criticism are involved. Internally, missed opportunities and deadlines, occasional dips in morale, periodic loss of faith and trust, and the plight of many young children and families seem more pronounced as we hold ourselves to increasingly higher standards.

But the occasional pats on the back and recognition from outside the school feel more meaningful and satisfying because we have overcome obstacles to reach them. They have greater power to sustain the effort and commitment to our mission. Getting it right, for me and for our school, no longer means only satisfying external requirements for what we should do. It means creating a community of like-minded people willing to risk disappointment in order to create—and work toward—a common vision for success.

The school

Gardendale Elementary Magnet School (GEMS) is located eight miles from the entrance to NASA's Kennedy Space Center on Florida's east-central coast. The school was built in 1966 to accommodate growing enrollment resulting from the burgeoning space industry. Thus, Merritt Island became one of the county's major bedroom communities for many of the space center families. Enrollment at the school quickly grew to 1200 students. By 1978, when I became principal, however, a variety of social, economic, and demographic factors had reduced the enrollment to 400, 65 percent of whom were minority. Enrollment continued to decline for the next decade to a low of 240 students.

We were a school skidding toward failure and even closure. Making the absolute best of the often trying and difficult circumstances that we encountered, our faculty and parents gradually began to pull together. The staff displayed a willingness to try new ideas to improve upon its reality. We slowly sought and often found cause for optimism in the reform movement of the late 1980s and 1990s. The culture of getting it right is reflected in the school motto: "Today's dream is tomorrow's reality."

Gardendale Elementary School became the Brevard County School District's first and only single-tract year-round school in 1991. It opened its doors as Gardendale Elementary Magnet School in the fall of 1992, becoming the district's first and only elementary magnet school. Enrollment grew exponentially and in three years reached its program design capacity of 700. There has been a waiting list for each year since the inception of the magnet program.

Achievement test scores have improved dramatically and, in 1994, GEMS received the Florida Education Commissioner's Award as a Break-the-Mold School. In 1995 the school was selected by *Redbook* magazine as one of America's top six innovative schools. In 1996 it was designated a Magnet School of Merit by Magnet

Schools of America and in 1997 was named a Magnet School of Distinction. A description of the school's design and programs can be found in an article in the September 1995 issue of *Educational Leadership* titled "A GEM of a Choice" (Narvaez, 1995).

The progressive improvement of our school has brought me great satisfaction over my nearly twenty years at Gardendale. I would never have realized these rewards without a long-term commitment to staying at and with my school. I am immensely proud of the awards, recognitions, media coverage, and endless stream of international, national, and state visitors that have brought affirmation to our staff as they share with others the results of their efforts. For me as principal, however, there are other, more subtle events that provide me the sustenance to stay on and reinvigorate my leadership.

I've got my nine

At the inception of the magnet program, we reached consensus on how best to approach the problem of insufficient parental involvement in the school. We decided to require each family to volunteer nine hours each year at the school. We incorporated this agreement into the three-party (parent, student, school) agreement signed upon enrollment. We fully realized that there was no legal basis for enforcing the agreement and that our efforts might be better spent helping parents, for whom volunteering was uncomfortable, to be successful themselves. Expanding the definitions of volunteering, creating opportunities, recognizing volunteers' efforts, and nurturing our expectations for involvement has resulted in a five-year average of 90 percent participation in the nine-hour requirement.

A notebook rests in the front office in which parents record their hours of volunteer time. The notebook is on a counter not too far from my office. Late one afternoon, two parents returning from a field trip they had chaperoned came in to record their hours in the book. As I sat at my desk working, I could hear their banter on how well the trip had gone as they thumbed through the notebook to find the right page on which to record their hours. At that point one parent asked, with apparent pride, "Hey, I got my nine, do you have your nine?" I froze in mid-thought when I realized that this simple question reflected a very important part of the culture we were creating at the school and that our efforts were not in vain. I occasionally ask folks if they have their nine and 90 percent of the time the answer is affirmative with mixed tones of pride and matter-of-factness.

I often remember this experience when I reflect on the important role human beings play as enablers. I recall, too, that we drew these parents in by requiring them, when their children came to the school, to commit themselves to being here with us, too. By risking this requirement, we discovered a powerful force that has been essential to our school's success.

The colored paper incident

Our magnet school houses four schools within one building. The four teacher leaders who made up our leadership team and I had realized that regular written communication to parents from a variety of sources was taking place. The school newsletter, the PTO newsletter, official correspondence, a quarterly newsletter from each of the four schools, and a variety of newsletters and information from the classrooms were flowing from the school. In order to assist parents in sorting out this correspondence, we decided to assign a colored stationery to each of the newsletters.

I promptly drafted a memo to teachers outlining the color scheme and initiated procedures to purchase a modest supply of paper to start the process. Within two weeks my mailbox, at No. 1 Principal Place, was inundated with letters from students in our Microsociety School. This is the group that operates the postal system, bank, and city works where taxes are collected. They also operate "The Big Blues," our collection bins for recyclable paper. Their letters addressed a variety of environmental concerns, expressed in a variety of ways, about my colored paper directive.

Apparently they had learned that colored paper and the ink it requires excluded the paper from being recycled. They wanted the colored paper edict rescinded.

I fussed and fretted for several days as images of a school without any colored paper entered my mind. Finally, in a rational moment, I decided to meet with a delegation from the "resurgents." They were eloquent and passionate in their concerns and I quickly realized that this concern was not only serious but had the potential for a real-life learning experience. Despite their arguments, however, I was not convinced that all colored paper could not be recycled. I challenged the group to continue their research to see if they could come up with a compromise solution to the problem. I put them in contact with our district print shop and provided them the name of several paper manufacturers.

Several weeks later I was summoned to a classroom meeting. Seating had been rearranged so that I faced the panel; the remainder of the class and their proud teacher were the audience. Each panel member had his or her research notebook open and the panel chair handed me a notebook. The title page read "Executive Summary: Prepared for Mr. Narvaez—Our Findings and Recommendations." The seating and notebook most certainly heightened my anticipation of what was to come and my concern as to how I might respond. Each member of the panel proceeded through the content of the notebook. They had contacted a variety of printers and manufacturers of colored paper. Copies of phone logs and written correspondence were available, along with other research data. They had also contacted recycling centers and recorded their findings.

I was very impressed by the thoroughness of their work and the serious and professional manner of their presentation. But visions of the school without colors continued to haunt me. As they reached the point where conclusions of findings were being reported, much to my surprise, the panel focused on the chemical qualities that made certain colored papers nonrecyclable. Apparently, certain metal-based coloring agents retard the recycling process. Much to my relief, however, these eight- to ten-year-olds had located manufacturers of colored paper who used recyclable coloring agents in the manufacturing of their paper. My visions of a school with color began to return.

As the panel reported their recommendations, I was beset by another worry: How much is this going to cost me? Again, I was impressed by the soundness of their judgment. In short, they agreed that the existing supply of paper be utilized and that all future purchases be made from the most cost-effective manufacturer of the "right" paper.

After several questions from me were dispatched with ease, I praised and thanked the group for their work and diligence and exited with a promise to return with my decision. I had, of course, already made up my mind but wanted to crunch the numbers. I returned several days later to inform the classes that I had taken their recommendations and adopted the new school policy forthwith. The victory cheers were jubilant as the students realized that their vision had become a reality.

I often remember this experience when I reflect on the notion of inspiring and empowering children to have more say in what and how they can apply what they learn. I think we so often underestimate human potential, particularly that of children. My role as principal carries with it so much power to teach, to inspire, and to empower!

Am I doing all right?

The tremendous growth in enrollment at GEMS created a need to recruit, train, nurture, and assimilate new faculty into our school. In planning for this growth, the staff developed job descriptions so that prospective faculty would have some idea about our program and expectations. Teacher teams were involved in the interview process and I often took new hires back to their universities with me on recruitment trips. Although this process is time-consuming for many of us, I have come to see it as one of our most essential activities. It is where we begin investing in ourselves.

It was thus that a young man named Charles joined our faculty in January of 1994. He had been interviewed by a team at his university and anxiously awaited the opportunity to visit our school and be interviewed further. It was obvious to everyone that he had a genuine regard and respect for children and an almost compulsive desire to teach. Over the past three years, Charles has matured into one of the finest teachers I've known. Already in his short career, he has been recognized statewide for his teaching in the area of Law-Related Education. He is the subject of a collection of case studies of exemplary teachers. He has also become our chief recruiter at his former university. More important, he is liked and respected by everyone who has the opportunity to meet, work with, or learn from him.

Investing in Charles, however, required trust, patience, and commitment from us. The first year and a half of Charles's teaching was characterized by an almost daily quest for feedback, insight, support, and affirmation for his teaching. No one was immune from his queries: "How do you do this?" "How can I find out about that?" "What do think about this idea?" "Why didn't this work?" "Do you think they will like what I'm doing?" "Will they really understand this?" "Did I handle that all right?" Charles was working at getting it right.

His enthusiasm was infectious. "I just love teaching!" he would say. Or he'd volunteer, "I think this is a great school! I love being here!" We all heard him exclaim numerous times, "I can't think of anything I'd rather do than teach! I hope I'm becoming a good teacher!" Indeed, he was growing by leaps and bounds. His energy and delight became an inspiration for us. So did his obvious quest for improvement. Almost every Friday, and some weeks more often, he would pop his head into my office or stop me in the hallways and in all seriousness and in a variety of ways, ask, "Am I doing all right?" At first, his questions astounded me for their directness and sincerity. As I became accustomed to them, I would try to point to something specific that he was doing well. At one point, his requests for feedback almost became a problem because I was running out of ways to say how pleased I was with his teaching. The questions come far less frequently now. When they do, they are far more focused and reflective on the issues of the day. I now relish the occasional "Am I doing all right?"

These first years of Charles's teaching have set an interesting standard for me as I look at the development of teachers who join our faculty. I call it the Charles Factor. I listen intently to all conversations, questions, and interchanges for the various forms we all use to ask, "Am I doing all right?" I am seldom disappointed as I realize that everyone, in his or her own way, seeks and needs the approval of others in order to grow. One of my greatest rewards as principal came from nurturing my colleagues' growth with authentically felt approval and appreciation.

The eighteen years I've spent at Gardendale have formed me as an educator, as a leader, and as a person. Not only has each experience taught me something, but the continuity of those experiences has cumulatively shaped my assumptions, beliefs, and visions about what schools and people are and can be. Staying at one school for nearly two decades, I have witnessed the fruits of my labors and have come to understand my own influence.

All principals I meet and talk to have war stories to share. The most fascinating stories are those in which the principal takes the most adverse of situations and finds a silver lining that results in some form of victory. I believe we should nurture this ability to remember, reflect, and learn so that we can grow and move on to other challenges. Putting down roots in one school gives us the gift of time—time to see the silver lining, to appreciate the slow but sure pace of school improvements, and to form the relationships with parents, students, and staff so crucial to our success. Time also cushions us through all the short-term ups and downs and keeps us focused on the distant goal of some day getting it right.

Reference

Narvaez, Albert, Jr. "A GEM of a Choice." *Educational Leadership*, 1995, 52 (1), 9–11.

AL NARVAEZ *is principal of Gardendale Elementary Magnet School, Merritt Island, Florida.*

*A long-time elementary school principal captures in anecdote
the humor and humanity of his work with children.*

4

A few big lessons from a
few small teachers

Phil Hunsberger

IT WAS A WEEKDAY, a warm September day, as Teddy and I stood
outside Franklin Elementary School and watched the eleven buses
loaded with students pull away from the school. Teddy was a fourth
grader, one of the 265 students who started the 1982 school year
at Franklin. I was the principal. Teddy was riding his bike that day.

"Teddy, you know that if you ride your bike tomorrow, I'll need
a note."

"OK, Mr. H."

The two of us waved as the buses pulled out of the parking lot.
Once they were gone, Teddy took off on his bike, giving me a wave.

"Don't forget, tomorrow a note."

In 1982 95 percent of the Franklin students were bussed to
school. So it certainly was reasonable to me that if anyone were to
ride a bike to school, I would need the assurance of a note from the
parent. To me as the principal, such rules were reasonable, serving
meaningful purposes. My days were filled with the business of making them work.

The next day found Teddy and me back at the same spot to
watch the buses roll away. This time as I finished my wave to the
departing students, I turned to Teddy, expecting my note. With a
smile that displayed Teddy's obvious pride, he pulled from his

NEW DIRECTIONS FOR SCHOOL LEADERSHIP, NO. 5, FALL 1997 © JOSSEY-BASS PUBLISHERS

pocket a tiny slip of paper. Handing it to me, he said: "Here you go, Mr. H., see you tomorrow."

I watched Teddy pull out of the parking lot and head for home. I too was smiling. A reasonable rule and a thoughtful student's compliance were reasons for a young principal to feel a bit of pride. Then I read the note:

> MR. HUNSBERGER,
> I'M RiDiNG MY BiKE TODAY.
> TEDDY

I have kept that note in my wallet for the past fifteen years as a reminder to myself to be clear and specific. Teddy and his note were a great lesson for my leadership. As I now reflect upon my sixteen years as a building principal, Teddy was only one among many students who taught me some valuable lessons about leadership.

The Inuit believe that each of us is endowed with strengths that are also our lessons. Strengths and lessons, an intriguing partnership. The Inuit also believe that a strength is only a disguise for a lesson. An intricate relationship exists between the strength and the lesson. In short, a strength can only be considered an asset if it is used to improve our culture. Thus the lesson of the strength is the manner in which we use it.

Teddy kindly put me in touch with one of those lessons in leadership leading to strength. That is, in our complicated world it is essential that our messages are delivered with clarity. Teddy brought a note. He behaved exactly as my message requested and it was I who failed to make plain to him what my message intended.

How many countless "goofs" in our school business emerge from an unclear message? How many times have we lost an opportunity because of writing that is either too obscure or too convoluted? From that day out watching the buses to this, I have truly strived to ensure that my messages clearly communicate my meanings. For this reason, I hold a fondness for Teddy. He was a wonderful teacher without knowing either the value of his lesson or the gratitude I would feel for his gift. Thanks, Teddy!

Jason was a first-grader. His teacher came to me in 1988 and said, "Phil, I don't know what to do with Jason. He reads. I mean he reads anything. I mean he reads everything." I noted a certain panic in her voice, so I said, "Well, I'd like to listen to Jason read." So, on one afternoon in the library of Franklin School I listened to this pudgy little boy with thick glasses read Shel Silverstein to me. Shel was just one of the favorite books in a grocery bag that he brought to read to me. We spent at least an hour in that library. Jason read fluently, with understanding, and with an absolutely real attachment to the author's words. More important, as I watched Jason read I saw him own the stories. An amazing connection existed between Jason and those poems and stories. He laughed aloud. He sighed with relief. His face showed worry, exuberance, and delight. It was not merely that he was reading words; Jason was a part of the writing.

Sure, Shel Silverstein provided the comical drawing and marvelous plays on words. Jason, however, was more than simply entertained. He was not only the reader of the poem, he completed the picture. A poem has no meaning without an audience. A story has no purpose without someone to believe it. Jason made complete the purpose of writing. He was more than a participant; in fact, he became a major character, owning the writing.

I was stunned.

I also decided I wanted some part of this action! I could write poetry. I could write stories. I could share this with my students. I could create that same sense of connection that Jason had with his grocery bag of books for all of our 235 students. I invented a playground dragon. I introduced my students during lunch to the wizard who lived in the Franklin roof. For our kindergarten students I wrote a poem that I turned into a song about dinosaurs coming to school: "I wonder if they'll be buying lunch? I wonder if my tables they'll crunch? And wouldn't it be a horrible fuss if I have to let them ride the bus? Oh me, oh my, what in the world do I do? Now I've got kids and dinosaurs all coming to school!" I wrote and shared. As I did, I discovered another one of those strengths. The children coming to school at Franklin had something no one else had: a playground dragon, a song about dinosaurs, and a wizard. When I left Franklin and went to Jefferson, I introduced those children to R. M. Cutwater, a leprechaun who lived in the tunnel beneath the school.

All of these stories and poems added up to a kind of folklore, a schoolhouse folklore allowing children to be more than just students of a school. They became players in a fantasy and it gave them a special kind of ownership of their school—a kind that only children could feel and believe. And it all started with Jason.

Yesterday afternoon, I was walking the hallways in our high school. It was one of the first sunny days of spring, when the air turns warm and students no longer wish to be students. I walked into a class and saw some of my former students. They said, "Mr. H., does R. M. Cutwater still eat erasers?" I smiled. "Sure he does," I replied. Thanks, Jason!

One little kindergarten girl, Christy, put me in touch with the strength of invitation. It was Christy's very first day of school at Franklin School. I chose that particular morning to open all the doors of our school. It was no big deal (except for all the flies that took advantage of the open doors!). Later, I learned from Christy's mother about her first day. She told her mother, "And you know what, Mom, the door was wide open for me."

A five-year-old sees a door open only for her. She decides that school is an inviting place. How often do we recognize that responsiveness to our children need not be fanfare and glitz? Indeed, there are quite simple actions that carry a most positive message. Open a door.

I found that sense of invitation and responsiveness too in a student named Jackie. A family full of compassion, love, and an abundant store of good will adopted Jackie, enrolling her as a kindergartner in Franklin School. Jackie was eligible for special education services from the start. Over all seven of her elementary years in Franklin School, I watched as she navigated the struggles of learning. Like other special needs students, her successes were made up of small steps forward and, periodically, large steps backward. However, Jackie was surrounded by people who cared: her teachers, her family, her friends, and her principal.

About two weeks ago, having not seen Jackie for over ten years, I received a card in the mail. It was from Jackie. Her mother had written this note: "Jackie talks about you often and has realized all these years that you were one who always 'noticed' all students no matter how smart or not-smart they were. She always responded to a cheerful attitude of those around her. When she was shopping the other day she wanted this card and I asked for who? She said "Mr. Hunsberger"—so here it is." The card simply said: "Without your friendly smiling face . . . it's just not the same old place." Jackie's signature in shaky manuscript had for me a certain eloquence. I was touched.

How simple empowerment can be: an open door, a quick and ready smile. Leadership through unrelenting optimism can be such a meaningful strength. Often this strength is criticized as naive and simply a view through rose-colored glasses. However, my small teachers would suggest the opposite. Thanks, Jackie.

Jake taught me how to juggle. The object of juggling is to keep things moving, like tossing balls or spinning plates. The effort is to time the catches, keep the sequence active, and keep the object in the air. Jake's lesson used neither the plate nor the ball, however. I soon discovered his "objects."

One morning while I was walking through the hallway I heard a rather strange noise from a locker and, opening the locker to investigate, was greeted with three kittens in a book bag. It was Jake's locker and the three kittens were for his Show and Tell. Unfortunately, Show and Tell was in the afternoon, so these kittens were simply renting space until their grand appearance. How he managed to hide the kittens from his parents as he left for school, hide them on the forty-minute bus ride, and get them to his locker (overcoming the temptation to display them to his friends!) was a bit beyond my thinking. Standing there in the hallway, none of this mattered. I needed to have a talk with Jake.

Ensconced in my office with Jake and his kittens, my lesson in juggling was about to begin. I was a young principal and a most novice juggler. Imagine the scene as the Director of Fine Arts greeted me at the office door for our early morning meeting! I am on the floor corralling the kittens toward the box. Two are establishing territory while I'm coaxing the other to sip the milk strategically placed in the box. Jake is still whimpering and negotiating with me his rights for Show and Tell. My secretary is waiting for me to make the morning announcements. I now am faced with every juggler's nightmare. Just which of these plates must I let drop?

I chose to drop the "punishment" one, the one that would have dealt a stringent consequence for Jake's obviously poor behavior. Jake was simply solving the problem of an afternoon Show and Tell. He was a compassionate young lad who would never hurt his animals intentionally. He solved his dilemma with what he felt to be an appropriate action. Instead of punishment, Jake and I had several reading sessions over the next few weeks about proper animal care.

Jake did teach me the strength of leadership that can be achieved through really effective juggling. A principal's life is filled with dilemmas, complications, situations, and considerations. As each of these enters the office, it carries with it a sense of urgency or even emergency and the unfortunate belief that an absolute immediate answer is available. Leadership is the skill of keeping all these things in some kind of order and keeping some kind of reasonable perspective without dropping the plate. Thanks, Jake. I suppose this lesson could have been introduced with a bit less commotion from you and your kittens, but I'm not sure without them I would have learned it!

In 1993, after I had left the principalship to take a central office position as the Director of Student and Staff Services, I met another important teacher. Jimmy is autistic. He was a second-grade student in one of our elementary schools. His mother was a strong advocate of Jimmy's rights to a normal educational experience. She was a valiant crusader for Jimmy's well-being and fought for his opportunity to participate as any other second-grader in public schools. I became involved when both Jimmy's mother and the school had reached an impasse. All the righteousness of those who favored inclusivity confronted the frustrations of those who wondered, What can we really do? It was a time of anguish, a time in which all the players—mother, teacher, and principal—were confused by the apparent absence of a next step.

What could I do? I thought we might begin with Jimmy and his autism. As much as we did not know Jimmy, Jimmy did not know us. So we began with a series of conversations. Mom and I began with simple conversations about Jimmy. What he knew, what he did, and what we hoped he could do became the context for our conversations. The advantage we had with conversation was that no decisions had to be made. Jimmy's mother and I began to build a relationship rooted not in decisions but instead in understandings. Our conversations began to include more of the players: the teachers, the principal, and the advocates. Eventually, these folks made up the team that would begin to build an individual educational program (IEP) for Jimmy. The foundation of that IEP would be this belief: we will not ask Jimmy, an autistic child, not to be Jimmy, an autistic child.

Jimmy came carrying a tennis racket to a school built like a baseball diamond. Our challenge was to reshape the diamond so that it was more like a court for Jimmy. Our lessons grew immensely as we began to discover all of what Jimmy could teach us about learning. We created a nomenclature, which we called "student-at-large," which allowed Jimmy to float from second to third grade for appropriate learning experiences. We devised a behavior plan that was focused on dignity, protecting Jimmy's need to relate with his peers in a positive, humane fashion. We stretched all the boundaries to provide for the needs of this special soul. In the stretch, we discovered a broader sense of what learning and growth may indeed mean.

Phil Jackson, in his book *Sacred Hoops*, writes: "Inevitably, paradoxically, the acceptance of boundaries and limits is the gateway to freedom" (1995, p. 7). Jimmy put not only me but others in touch with the strength of pushing those boundaries. True, we will still need to find ways for Jimmy to stay connected with us as he grows up, but how much about learning have we already learned from

Jimmy? Jimmy's mother now is our advocate and is a valiant crusader for the possibility of our working together. Though not all teachers will agree that a very special IEP written for Jimmy has implications for all learners, there are those who now explore the possibilities beyond the borders of grade levels, assessment, and traditional learning experiences. Thanks, Jimmy, you taught me the strength of questioning the norm and exploring the frontiers beyond the boundaries.

Mendy had written *The Lie* as a high school entry for the nonfiction category of our literary magazine. Her story recounts a time when she was in first grade and decided that she could cut her own bangs. Needless to say, her mother, who was a beautician, was not pleased with her decision. So Mendy fabricated a cover story in which a bully sixth grader had cut her hair at recess. Her story eventually led to my inclusion in the real incident (and a third-place award in the contest). She wrote:

As I walked through the classroom door, there stood Mr. Hunsberger. With a friendly "Hello," he politely asked me to walk with him to his office. Stiff as a board, I followed him all the way down the hall. As we passed the chorus room, he asked me if I had anything I would like to explain. Weeping in quiet tears, I slowly retold the mistaken truth and admitted to him what had really happened.

I could tell by his face as we sat in his office that he had known all along there was no way some sixth grader would have trapped me into a corner just to cut my hair. Word by word, sigh by sigh, the truth came out. All he had wanted was to help me get the real truth out. Mission accomplished, right? Not quite. There was still my mother. As I sat in Mr. Hunsberger's office, he made me call my mother and tell her everything.

How often do leaders take on the task of leading people to truth? A tough path indeed in today's complex world. Though some truths are rather easy to spot, as was Mendy's feeble attempt to reshape a particularly bad decision, our world of education grows excessively complex. Finding truth is a bit like weaving through obscurity. Nonetheless, that's what principals do.

My small teachers put me in touch with strengths, and, as the Inuit believe, with lessons that I continue to live by. As I review my principalship, these lessons are some of the most precious rewards. As I have gained from this sometimes frustrating work with my small teachers, so they have gained from the lessons of my school. I know this because I have followed the lives of many of our students. Although I have lost touch with Teddy and Jake, I can report on the others.

Jason has a fellowship as a graduate student in the creative writing program at the Ohio State University. It will be no surprise to me if eventually we are all reading his stories; he now completes that writing picture from a different side!

Christy just finished her first year at the University of Wisconsin, Madison as a microbiology major. I imagine that on that massive campus a sense of invitation may be somewhat fleeting. However, I'm sure her self-esteem and confidence will readily open those doors.

Jackie is still living with her family. She recently recovered from a massive stroke that caused one of those tremendous steps backward. However, she will graduate from high school next year. Her family will undoubtedly treat Jackie's graduation as a twenty year old with the same celebration and pride they did with their other children.

I thanked Mendy during her fourth-hour English class yesterday for including me in her story. I also congratulated her for her third-place award.

"So, Mendy," I wondered, "when you graduate, what do you intend to do?" Mendy smiled, turned a bit red, and replied, "I'm going to be a beautician."

"Most likely, a very good one, too," I said.

Jimmy is still teaching! We recently met to begin the transition from the elementary school to the middle school. It should be exciting to see the reshaping we do on that baseball diamond. On the other hand, Jimmy has been learning how to hold a bat, catch a ball, and he even runs a few bases!

My leadership as a principal benefited greatly from the value I placed on clear communication, unrelenting optimism, keeping a proper perspective, leading folks toward truth, and a continual willingness to push at boundaries. Isn't it remarkable that the children rewarded me with such lessons!

Reference

Jackson, P. *Sacred Hoops: Spiritual Lessons of a Hardwood Warrior*. New York: Hyperion, 1995.

PHIL HUNSBERGER *was a principal for seventeen years and is currently Director of Human Resources for Community Unit School District 5 in Sterling, Illinois.*

*A high school principal explores her evolution as a leader by
examining the "ripples" she has helped to make in her schools.*

5

Throwing rocks in the pond

Fran Vandiver

ALL OF US as children probably stood by a pond and threw a rock
into the water to watch the concentric circles that inevitably followed. I can remember throwing rocks that were progressively
heavier to see if the circles lasted longer with the heavier rocks.
Principals have opportunities that are very similar to throwing
rocks into the pond. We don't really throw rocks but we do have
the opportunity to toss out new ideas, procedures, questions, sym-
bols, and ceremonies in an effort to make ripples in our schools.
We don't usually have many ponds on campus, either, but we do
have our school's culture and the context of activities that surrounds
us on a daily basis.

The "rocks" I throw into the cultural context of my school are
aimed at celebrating adults as well as students. I find it a constant
challenge to stay focused on teaching and learning while in the
usual swirl of activities, district mandates, daily crises, and assorted
pressures. I stay at it because when all is said and done, I have
learned how to recognize and appreciate my "ripples."

In trying to understand what drives me to be a principal—what
keeps me at it daily—it is first necessary to understand that being a
principal was never a long-range goal for me. I wanted to be a teacher
and I had wanted to be a teacher for a long time. My motivation was

NEW DIRECTIONS FOR SCHOOL LEADERSHIP, NO. 5, FALL 1997 © JOSSEY-BASS PUBLISHERS

fueled by the many wrongs I had witnessed as a student. I had worked with children from the age of twelve as a baby-sitter, a camp counselor, a coach, and a tutor. As I watched students being treated with a lack of respect and saw how they reacted when humiliated, it deepened my resolve to become a teacher and use the influence that I would have as a teacher in a positive way. I also just enjoyed being around kids and watching them develop. I knew I wanted to work with secondary students and I set off to do just that.

I began my career as a physical education teacher, coach, and social studies teacher. I taught in junior high, high school, middle school, private higher education, and community college outreach programs. However, it wasn't until serving as a department chairman that I realized I could influence curriculum and instruction for more students than merely my own. My first glimpse of that truth was when I went to a county department meeting in place of my department chair. I heard all kinds of information that I had never heard before and realized that the "stuff" that is sent to the department chairs was a potential source of information and growth for all the teachers in the department. I could see that if this information were shared with the other teachers and if we worked together, it could help our own teaching and, consequently, our students' learning.

During the time I was a department chair, our department worked together to coordinate themes, share ideas, and get to know each other better. Of course, this was long before the literature began to talk about collaborative cultures and learning communities. It just seemed to make sense that if we knew what each of us was doing, if we shared information and planning, and if we knew who we were as people, we could have a greater impact on students—and enjoy it more. Encouragement from my principal to widen my scope of influence led me to seek certification in administration and supervision. I was a middle school assistant principal for three years and a middle school principal for six-and-a-half years before becoming the principal of a high school two years ago.

Sharing decision making? What do you make of it?

I have struggled through the evolution of shared decision making, and though it was complicated and personally challenging for me and for staff, this rock has led to many sustained ripples. Our middle school was part of a pilot program to explore shared decision making. For the first year, I struggled with what my role as principal should be: how was I to begin sharing?

I adopted a nonparticipative role at staff meetings because I thought my not being THE LEADER was an important first step to sharing decision making. I did not purposefully run the meetings and I consciously did not participate actively in the initial conversations because I did not want to appear to think I knew more or was pushing my agenda. I did not meet with the chairperson to help her set the meeting agendas. Because I did not know what the agenda items were, I did not provide her with information that would have allowed her to be more effective and knowledgeable. Because we were not meeting, there was no processing of the meetings, no discussions as to the direction the meetings should take, and very little continuity. Understandably, both of us grew more and more frustrated as the year moved on.

One day as we were about to talk about the next meeting, I decided that I just had to tell her how miserable I was with the process. Speaking openly about this allowed her to also express her frustrations. She felt she was inadequate for the job; she didn't know what to do and ended up doing almost everything alone. I felt that I had some of the information and good facilitating skills that could help the Council grow and change but did not comment out of fear of LEADING. We began talking about, analyzing, and reflecting on our roles and about where we were and where we should be.

Thereafter, we collaborated on meeting agendas and direction. I made a conscious decision to be an active participant, to acknowledge that I was the principal and that, among other things, I did have access to more information, a wider scope of influence, and often a broader perspective than most others. I worked on feeling comfortable that those were the areas of expertise that I brought to our shared decision-making process. Our mutual confession led to mutual trust and to a new form of collaborative leadership at the school.

I began to realize that I could not pretend not to have information that I actually had. I realized that I could participate without dominating. Even with shared decision making, the principal is still the principal. Through an agenda that legitimized questioning, allowed for the confronting of ideas, and invited participation from all the members, I was able to participate freely and openly and to be a legitimate member of the group. For the first time, I felt that I could do this from who I am and what I know. I had a horrible misconception that, to have shared governance, I had to somehow relinquish who I was and what I knew in order to let the teachers feel free to participate in the process. What I had done was frustrate others and myself.

Sharing decision making has been rewarding for me because I have found affirmation of myself as a leader. Changing my role as principal meant changing my relationship with teachers, but it did not mean losing my identity. It meant expanding that identity to encompass more people, information, and skills into the leadership and decision-making process at the school. Learning that valuable lesson several years ago has allowed me to continue to develop my skills in shared leadership. That has been immensely productive for the school and fulfilling for me. As teachers realize that they can make important decisions about curriculum, instruction, assessment, and scheduling, for example, they realize that there is no THEY that won't let US do what we want. We *are* they.

Learning is for everyone

Eliminating old barriers brings uneasiness and uncertainty. One morning in October during my first principalship, two excellent veteran teachers came by my office and stood in the doorway. (I had noticed that teachers often stood in the doorway, as if there was quicksand in the room.) They looked at each other and one of them said, "You know, we're not used to making decisions around here." The other teacher added something like, "Yeah, Fran, we think that you should slow down." Since that day nearly ten years ago, I have heard these same words many times in some form or another. Rather than scaring me, they always reassure me that more folks understand that school decision making is a *we* activity and not an *I* activity. They also remind me that change is unsettling and makes novices of all of us. Being unsettled without knowledge, direction, or focus develops tension and frustration. Being unsettled but having knowledge, direction, and focus develops creative tension. It is this state of creative tension that allows new ways of looking at old problems and the development of new solutions.

I also learned to acknowledge that change made me, the principal, a novice, too; I was not always certain of what needed to be done. During my second year as a middle school principal, this realization led me to go back to school to increase my capacity to be an effective leader in our change process. At one of our faculty meetings, I told the faculty how I felt and that I was going to begin working on my doctorate and would be sharing with them as I learned. I told them that it would take a community effort to provide success for all students, that we all had to learn more than we already knew, and that I was making my commitment to do that.

Although standing in front of your faculty and acknowledging that you need to continue to learn might be considered risky, for me it was one of the most liberating events that I have experienced as a principal. By leveling the playing field, becoming the "head learner," and expecting that all of us would learn together how best to craft our school, it freed us to say we didn't know something and to learn with and from each other.

Now that I am at a high school, I have had the opportunity to throw that rock into the pond again. Once again, I have discovered how much I did not know and how much I have yet to learn about high school. The worlds of tech-prep, graduation requirements, rotating schedules, dual enrollment, twenty-two varsity sports, and countless activities were all foreign to me. Everyone in the school and many others have helped me get up to speed. In the past two years, we have developed a four-year restructuring plan, moved to a 4×4 block schedule, crafted a new program for ninth graders who enter without the skills needed to be successful, and provided multiple opportunities for adult learning.

We have accepted the challenge to craft our school to provide success for all students. This expectation does raise the bar for all of us in the school, but our belief that we can learn sustains us all in our work to make positive changes in ourselves, our school, and our students' learning. The reward for my learning is that our students are progressing!

Students benefit when teachers create

My experience has taught me that when I am willing to risk sharing decision making and when I expect adult learning, there is a direct impact on student success. I have seen teachers become more confident through their continuous learning and become more understanding of the learning process that their students are also experiencing. I have watched teachers move from running dictatorial classrooms to planning collaborative ones as they make more decisions and are not told what do to. I have seen teachers edge away from the textbook-centered curriculum to a student-centered classroom as they learn how to take risks. I have listened to them as they celebrate the new enthusiasm they see in their students. I have heard students ask teachers, "Why can't you teach like Mrs. _____. She lets us DO STUFF!" For me, creating a culture in which teachers can create is most fulfilling. It takes me back to why I became an educator in the first place.

Willingness to take on challenges

Our social studies department provided an energizing experience for me when they decided they did not want to adopt the new

American history textbook that was on the district list. I told them that if they did not want the book, they should design the course and bring me an alternative suggestion. They went off to think about it and came back declaring their willingness to take on this challenge. We built in time for them to work together, explore ideas, and involve students and parents in the planning. The teachers crafted a wonderful course focused on four essential questions that used multiple resources, including technology, with a focus on student projects and exhibitions of mastery. The usual eighth-grade American history textbook-driven course became an inquiry-based course entitled "Whose America Is It, Anyway?"

The challenge to create was the rock; this course became a ripple that was effective in opening the floodgates of creativity for others on the staff. They now had a living example of teaching and learning in a nontraditional way. For me it was a concrete reminder that when you give teachers the time, support, and freedom to find their own answers, they will do so. They will do it with an enthusiasm and dedication that only true ownership brings.

Learning to create time

One of the barriers that all of us face is time—or more precisely, the lack of it. When I was appointed to my first principalship in June 1988, I had the opportunity to send teachers to work with Bruce Joyce and Beverly Showers to hear about their models of teaching. While visiting with the group, I heard Bruce Joyce state repeatedly that we would have to learn how to create time because there just wasn't enough money available to buy all the time that was needed to retrain teachers.

Our middle school was built during the 1970s when the open classroom was the rage. Every set of four rooms had an accordion wall that joined two rooms and collapsible walls that would allow the pod of four rooms to be a giant open space. By the time I got there in 1988, file cabinets, tables, bulletin boards, and other more inventive items had all but closed these walls permanently. Everyone taught in his or her own space, and there was no joint use by teachers or students of the available space or resources.

I used Bruce Joyce's phrase, "We'll have to create time" many times over the years. I began to provide opportunities for the teachers to learn cooperative teaching strategies and to visit schools that were using a more collaborative approach than we were. I began to bring a substitute in for a day and to use that substitute in six different classes in order to provide an extra period consecutive to the teachers' planning periods so the teachers could begin to see how much they could do with a little extra planning time. Soon, they were figuring out how to do that within their own teaching teams.

Teachers have come up with unique ways to create time for themselves and other colleagues so they can take advantage of learning opportunities or engage in planning. My caveat has been that the work done in this found time must benefit the whole team. Teams learned how to involve the elective teachers in helping with field days and art projects. This challenge to create time served as a rock that unsettled the status quo of teaching in isolation. I was rewarded as I saw teachers engage parents, and other professionals outside the teaching field, as part of their students' learning experiences. Parents have taken part in assessment, curriculum development, and instruction.

Why has it taken so long for someone to care about us?

This past year I had the opportunity to structure a performance-based program for incoming ninth-graders who were below grade level in reading, writing, and math. This began with honest one-on-one conversations with individual students and their parents about the student's actual performance level in these areas. For the students in this program, it is not unusual for performance levels to be at the upper elementary or middle school levels. Once the shock of an honest assessment wore off and the students became involved in our intensive program, all of them progressed. Through our conversations, these students have come to see that this is their last chance to put in the academic time needed to give them a shot to graduate from high school.

The initial data is exciting as these traditionally truant and often-disciplined students are coming to school at a 95 percent rate and classroom discipline is not a major concern. They are, for the most part, appreciative of our efforts and earnest in their hard work to improve their abilities. They know that we will not accept failure and that we will help them to succeed. At the end of the first semester in a regular high school schedule, two-thirds of the students had at least a 2.0 average and two were on the B Honor Roll. We celebrate these accomplishments and show them a future through vocational counseling and field trips to various businesses.

Recently, after one such celebration, a student took me aside and pointedly asked, "Why has it taken so long for someone to care about us?" She went on to say that they all had known that they weren't performing at grade level for many years. Rather than feeling defensive at this student's question, I found it an exciting affirmation of the work our teachers had done crafting this unique program and of the sincerity of our students. I find my core belief reinforced that when given respect, appreciation, and a chance for success, most, if not all students will respond positively and grow from the experiences.

Many days I am tired. Trying to keep my school going while responding to the demands of the system within which my school sits is draining. Countless hours spent in countless meetings that cover countless details that count for nothing wear me down. I know that the challenge is to keep my focus on teaching and learning in spite of the tidal waves of bureaucratic deadlines, emergencies, and misguided directions. The paradox of trying to develop a democratic school that encourages questioning, participation by multiple stakeholders, and shared decision making within a hierarchical system that is neither flexible nor responsive sometimes has me thinking how easy it would be simply to manage and comply.

But when those thoughts creep into my mind, I think about the teachers I know who have grown and developed into effective leaders and the many students who have found success. I think about the quest to develop a context where decision making is shared, learning is expected of everyone, and student success is the central theme. Perhaps this is the greatest driving force of all—that the ripple caused by throwing those rocks into the pond influences many others to do the same in their own contexts as principals, teachers, students, staff, and parents.

FRAN VANDIVER *is principal of Ft. Lauderdale High School, Ft. Lauderdale, Florida. Fran and her school are active in the Coalition of Essential Schools.*

Leading a school engages us daily in essential human experi-
ence and in the spirited quest for answers to age-old questions
raised by our students and staff.

6

There's no doubt we're alive

Paul Bianchi

I HAVE BEEN a school head over half my life—the head of the same
school, no less. When some parents in Atlanta wanted to begin an
alternative school in the early 1970s, they had all the necessary
ingredients to get going—with the exception of students, teachers,
a building, and money! They broke this cycle of nothingness by
deciding first to hire a headmaster. Because there was no school,
hardly anyone, of course, applied for the post, and, in perfect form,
they chose me, a twenty-five-year-old with no administrative experience and only two years of teaching. Some principals grow on the
job. I literally grew up on the job.

Because growing up requires nourishment, it is reasonable to
conclude that something about the job has sustained me over the
years. Only recently have I begun to realize why this job has
worked for me. For the longest time I was like a fish unaware of the
temperature or the quality of the water surrounding me. Being
head of a school was what I did. I hopped out of bed every morning knowing that every day would be different, but I had very little consciousness of why and how this job I had stumbled onto just
a few years out of high school suited me. Sometime within the last
few years, I realized that this "school thing" was probably my life's

NEW DIRECTIONS FOR SCHOOL LEADERSHIP, NO. 5, FALL 1997 ©JOSSEY-BASS PUBLISHERS work. No, there wouldn't be any penthouse on the Upper East Side, swanky New Yorker lifestyle, or opportunities for government service protecting the barricades of American democracy. I realized that my universe would continue to be a schoolhouse. So, what is it that has sustained me for a quarter of a century as headmaster?

The tempo, the pulse, and the existential lunchbox

I have always loved the tempo and pulse of a school. Many people work in schools because they believe education is Important Work. It is important, I agree, but so are many other jobs. The rhythm of the work is what keeps me going. I sensed it the first day of student teaching in a suburban Boston high school. The energy of the hallways pulsates with current alternating between chaos and high purpose. School has always felt so alive that it keeps me feeling alive.

Although I can explain what I do and the institution I represent in the words of lofty goals and institutional mission statements, the job appeals to me most in the nitty-gritty, on the ground floor of daily experience. Two weeks ago a six-year-old boy, Sam, approached the receptionist outside my office and demanded to speak to the principal. He was upset, he said, because he heard that the art teacher had recently been fired and he didn't think he liked the new one. The receptionist peeked around the corner and said that I was available. "Why don't you go in and see him right now?" she offered. "Well, I really didn't want to talk to him in his office," Sam said. She coaxed him in anyhow. Sam rallied. He told me his concerns about the change in personnel, what the other kids were saying about the new teacher, and how he liked the former teacher. As an afterthought, he let slip that he actually had not yet been to art since the change, nor had he personally met the replacement. Ah, I thought, an opening. Sam and I spent the next fifteen minutes talking about how hard it was to go through change, to give someone new a chance, and to have the courage to say exactly what you believe to someone in charge.

We are all going to school with Sam, trying to find answers to these and other questions. I am always surprised by the number of reasonable grown-ups whose hands perspire and tongues knot up when they cross the threshold of the door to the principal's office. I am not a particularly imposing person, but often we are not reacting to who or what is before us, but rather to experiences behind us.

Every teacher and principal has a thousand Sam stories. Woven together they make up the fabric of our professional experience. Every day each of us brings to school the important issues of our own lives and of life itself, issues and questions that either do not have answers or do not have easy answers. Is there truth? What constitutes justice? What is the balance between authority and freedom? When do we compromise in life and when do we stick to our principles? What is the nature of individual differences? How do we respect diversity and learn to get along? How do we help others grow up? Who gets included in decision making and what difference does it make? These and other age-old questions, the stuff of Greek morality plays as well as sex, drugs, and rock 'n' roll, are the currency of our realm.

To paraphrase John Dewey, education isn't getting ready for life, it is life itself. The questions that swirl around the hallways and playground of every school are the same ones being asked by philosophers or anyone else who is trying to figure out how to live a good life. Batting them around is like playing in the major leagues with Aristotle or Buddha, only better. The players are kids like Sam, the teacher he misses who went sour on the vine, and the principal who couldn't figure out how to put a stop to the souring process. We each carry our existential lunch boxes to school every day and bump into each other, trying to figure out the rules of the game and play it at the same time.

The parts that need fixing

The imperfections of school life appeal to me and, in some perverse way, sustain me. Even before I hit the front door of the school each morning, I will see something that I think needs fixing—by me, by a teacher, by a family, or by all of us together. I know it is more fun to be around people who appreciate the part of the glass that is full, but it is the part that is empty—that needs filling—that motivates me. I like the emptiness because it is challenging and because it is humbling. It reminds me every day that there is more left to do, lots more, and that as well as we think we have our routine practices down at school, we can still do better.

When I first came to Atlanta, I taught at a school where the headmaster, Elliott Galloway, talked endlessly about Sisyphus. No matter what the topic, Elliott could work old Sisyphus into the conversation and remind us that in school all of us were just pushing that rock up the hill for all eternity. We snickered the snicker of young recruits listening to an old veteran's war stories but, in retrospect, Elliott and Sisyphus had something going for them. Sisyphus had what many people want: he had steady work. He didn't have to sit on the sidelines and he couldn't fool himself into believing that he had arrived. Complacency and the arrogance that surrounds it can be a slow and imperceptible death. Staying alive to the pitfalls and imperfections of school, as well the possibilities, is compelling.

Think how little fun it would be to play or watch baseball if lots of people batted a thousand. Thank God that Tony Gwynn hits into an out more than half the time. Good teaching is a good batting average, and a good school has a lineup of good hitters sensitive to the fact that they are playing on the same team. The batting average analogy, which I use often, is liberating because it frees us from being shackled to impossible, self-righteous standards of perfection. Most of us do our best work and have our greatest fun when we acknowledge to ourselves that it is an imperfect world we live in and that we will make mistakes.

A number of years ago a few teachers and I began a tradition at Paideia. We established a Screw-Up Hall of Fame for faculty and staff. Once a year, usually in the privacy of the Board-Faculty Christmas party, we stage a pageant where ten finalists from the past twelve months are announced and, like a beauty contest, a winner is crowned. Throughout the year nominations from faculty and staff pour into my office. I file them in a box on my desk discreetly mislabelled "Faculty and Administrative Issues." Anyone who works for the school is eligible. I have won the award twice myself (and am nominated with discouraging frequency). We have a plaque listing the winners through the years, but we don't display it in mixed company.

The rhetoric of most schools is often so deadening and misleading. Rarely does anyone speaking for the school acknowledge the limitations, the complexities, or the problems inherent in every school. The descriptions are about as false as the advertising brochures colleges send to prospective applicants. Such idealized and sanitized rhetoric reduces the possibility of honest dialogue about schools and school reform; even more important, it is self-deceiving. We begin to believe our own public relations, and being imprinted with false pictures of an idyllic world makes us less able to understand and act on the world as it is. Private schools, in my experience, are particularly susceptible to this self-deception. We kid ourselves, sometimes smugly, that the advantages of selectivity represent superior practice. We quote ourselves, repeat the motto from the school emblem, and confuse privilege with wisdom.

We did not establish the Screw-Up Hall of Fame as part of the school's mission statement. Nor was it an outgrowth of some overly processed administrative initiative. I'm sure the idea came out of the faculty lounge on a rainy day when just one too many things had gone wrong. But we have kept the tradition going because it represents an attitude that keeps us going, an attitude which acknowledges that our work is as complicated as life itself and that the potential for great folly and great achievement fills our days.

I have a framed poster in my office, a watercolor abstract from the artist Sister Corita Kent. The art is fine, but what I really like are the words from Zen scrawled at the bottom: "After ecstasy, the laundry." The expression represents the rollercoaster of events and emotions that are the high thrills and humbling reality of teaching and schoolmastering. Just when something really wonderful has happened, watch out; we are about to be hurtled down the perilous slope, screaming and out of control. Sisyphus' rock may even bop us as it goes tumbling by, and some day we will not be able to make it back up the incline to ecstasy. But in the meantime, it is a grand amusement park, we are on the best ride, and there is no doubt that we are alive.

What more could you ask?

PAUL BIANCHI *is the founding headmaster of The Paideia School in Atlanta, Georgia.*

A K–12 principal ponders the intricacies of power-sharing while staying true to himself. In so doing, he articulates universal tensions for all leaders.

7

My nonnegotiables

Barney Hallowell

THE BEST MEASURE of effective school leadership may be what works. At least, that has been the case with me. When I reflect on the satisfactions of my principalship, I return again and again to what has (and has not) worked for me. From what works, I have discovered that certain principles—my nonnegotiable essentials of school leadership—lie at the root of what rewards me in my work.

The first is that leadership is not singular, even though we like to pretend it is in certain specific instances; for example, when "the buck stops here," or when somebody has to take responsibility and be accountable. That may, in fact, be the outcome, the consequence, or the bottom line, as one superintendent liked to remind me. But that should not dictate the operative reality of effective leadership. Leadership is best when it is shared—genuinely done together. I do not always know where the buck stops, but I think I know where it best starts, and that is with *us*, rather than with you or with me.

Whenever I try to talk about this, I find myself sounding like a Milquetoast, abdicating, blurring, and confusing, but not taking responsibility for my leadership. I am the principal. Maybe a better way of saying it would be: I am the head leader in our school. But even that fails to fully capture it. My point is that I cannot do

NEW DIRECTIONS FOR SCHOOL LEADERSHIP, NO. 5, FALL 1997 © JOSSEY-BASS PUBLISHERS

the best job that can be done as leader without others who lead, without their intelligence, insight, ability, energy, understanding—without their leadership. And it is not enough for me to hold secretly to that ultimate notion of The Leader; I must let it go. If I cannot, others cannot truly lead. Our school, to be all it needs to be for our children, must have others who initiate, take charge, support, and work hard.

That brings me to a second and related nonnegotiable. To lead well, I must attract and surround myself with great people—great leader-learners. Again, maybe this is not a universal truth. I am sure there are leaders who can make people great, maximize their potential, and meld an effective working team from the people they inherit. I only know that I am not one of them. And if I tried to be, I would be setting myself up for frustration and failure. I think I have been able to inspire some people, even manage and counsel and guide them in creating a strong team. But I have come to believe that for our school to do the best job, ultimately I must rely on great people and it is important, perhaps even critical, to move those who are not going to be great out and bring strong leader-learners in.

This attitude has gotten me in trouble from time to time, but I am comfortable with my consistency on it. Weak teachers do not strong schools make. I have tried to not make decisions about weak people arbitrarily or capriciously. Nor have I made them unilaterally. I have tried to observe how well people work together and to assist those who are struggling; so have other leaders on our staff who have observed the same things and who might be more effective than I in supporting and counseling struggling colleagues. When there is that effort, made by many over a period of time, and the consensus is that an individual is not going to be great in our school, then leadership needs to change that situation, move that individual, bring in someone who is going to contribute to the important mission of the school.

Which leads to a third nonnegotiable. In terms of leadership in education, the vision—the commitment—must be clear and inviolate: schools are, first and foremost, about individuals—individual children, individual students, individual learners. They are not about buildings or school boards or money or power or sports or test scores. Because they are about students and learning, they are about teaching, as well. If we do not have great teachers, and if I do not make my primary objective to support, encourage, allow, and develop great teaching and great learning, then I am in trouble. If I allow my vision to become blurred, to rationalize poor teaching or poor administration for expediency or politics, I surrender my commitment to our students.

Finally, the nonnegotiable that I come back to most often is being true to myself—heeding the call of my heart, my core, for better or worse. Sooner or later, a true leader is going to stir the pot and, if great things happen as a result, is going to get splattered and slopped on. Spillage is inevitable. In this sense, the buck does stop here. If I truly believe in the vitality of what I am doing and that what *we* are doing is best for the students, then I can live with our decisions, despite the spillage. I must not ever stop listening to and hearing others; but I can only find peace with myself when I do what I believe, in the end, is right for the students.

All of this takes a lot of trust and self-assuredness. Yet, ironically, I believe that for leaders like me, *self doubt* is the critical grounding and balancing dynamic of my personality in my leadership style. Otherwise, I fear, I could easily become that singular leader, that captain, that purveyor of a "my way or the highway" philosophy. My self-doubt protects me against the idealized model of a leader as the tall, calm, unflappable, probably white-haired, supremely wise and deeply respected person who always knows and invariably does the right thing, whose charisma and demeanor command deference and understanding, whose inner strength, vision, and confidence are unquestioned. Despite my convictions to the contrary, I have discovered that I am driven to model myself after this idealized leader.

Ironically, I have found that I can succeed at many aspects of the ideal, using my self-confidence and charisma to exercise significant power over others. I think my self-doubt serves to keep my self-confidence and arrogance under control, a sort of balancing act that, when working well, can be constructive and productive, and when not working well can be disastrous. It is that awareness of potential disaster—the image of slipping off the high wire—that keeps me focused and in shape, trying to learn everything that I can about my craft and myself.

I need also explain that I believe that experience, fate, and chemistry have played, at least in my case, important roles in shaping me as a leader, and my journey toward *becoming* a leader, and cannot be separated out of this analysis. They don't qualify exactly as non-negotiables, but you cannot do it without them. Just as with great teaching, I believe that self questioning leadership—great leadership—is an art, an art that requires skill and training, but talent and passion, as well.

When I took over as principal six years ago in the summer of 1991, I was fueled by the confidence that I had some ideas about how to improve our school and how to provide some leadership. And, as well, by real self-doubt—that is, self-questioning—about whether I could pull it off. I felt a lot of pressure to succeed in the face of major challenges: discipline problems in the school, high teacher turnover, low student and teacher morale, a financial mess, a deteriorated and inadequate facility, a general sense of instability, and a lack of community support for the school. Students and the board, if not the community as a whole, held high, almost unreasonable expectations of me to get things done.

I made many, many mistakes. My lack of knowledge hit me very early. In fact, it was my growing awareness and realization of how little I knew that moved me toward the kind of open discussion and shared leadership approach we have today. I learned that true leadership was not about what I wanted or needed, but what the school needed, what teachers and students and parents needed, to make education work and be great. I learned the importance of seeing and listening to the leaders around me, especially the students and teachers. I eventually resolved that it is great teachers who make great schools, and that perhaps the single most important thing I could do is find, hire, and keep great teachers in our school.

It is much too easy for me to be glib about this lesson. "Discovering the leaders around me" seems naive and idealistic. The truth, though, is that it has been incredibly liberating and validating to empower teachers and students, to use the collective intelligence, talent, and energy of the school community to allow leadership to happen, rather than to control and limit it. In this sense, leadership means keeping the focus on what makes good education for kids and what it takes, with all of those other considerations, to accomplish it.

The tension between sharing leadership and championing my own ideas has nevertheless been a continuing struggle for me. On one hand, I have ideas about ways to do things and the authority to implement them; on the other, I realize that my way is not always, necessarily, the only right way. *Sharing* those ideas, *and the authority and power to get them done*, wasn't easy, but I eventually came to see that it was what worked for the school as well as for me.

This is where my nonnegotiables now lie: in what I believe, in what I do, in what I have learned as I understand leadership today. Talk the talk and walk the walk. As a person, as a teacher, and as a leader, I want to keep learning and reflecting and trying things out. I hope I do not ever think I have all the answers. I have learned a lot about effective principalship and great leadership, but know I have a lot more to learn. I am very aware that I am not a fully actualized leader and that I never will be. That is why I do not think that leadership in our school can ever be just about me, the principal, The Leader, even though the buck often does stop here. Maybe I will surprise myself. Maybe, some day, I will actually be that wise, white-haired, and singular leader (but I doubt it).

BARNEY HALLOWELL *is principal of a K–12 school on the island of North Haven, Maine.*

Gordon Nunemaker writes a weekly column on education that often vividly reflects his life as a principal. This chapter exudes the humor, warmth, and vitality he draws from his daily work as a leader.

8

On raccoons, Beatles, and relevance

Gordon Nunemaker

EACH CLASSROOM at my school is connected to the office by the public address system. If teachers need to contact the nurse, the secretary, or me, they just pull a cord. In the office, a small red light identifies the room, a soft "beep" sounds, and we talk.

More often than not, "beeps" do not herald good news. Some are the "could-you-send-a-custodian-with-a-mop-and-bucket" type. No further explanation needed. Others are the "I'm-sending-Sally-to-see-the-nurse" type. The custodian and his bucket better head this way. The more ominous "Mr.-N.-please-come-to-my-room" type can be just about anything. And when it's the "I'm-sending-Johnny-up-to-see-Mr. N." type, it's a safe bet that Johnny and I will not be discussing why the pokey little puppy was so pokey.

Speaking of puppies, there's also the principal's favorite, the "wildlife-warning" beep. I don't know what it is about kids and critters, but they seem to have a mutual attraction. Maybe animals just love being the center of attention. Whatever it is, you know that ten seconds after you hear, "Beep—Mr. N., there's a dog on the playground," you're going to hear, "Beep—Mr. N., there's a dog in the building."

NEW DIRECTIONS FOR SCHOOL LEADERSHIP, NO. 5, FALL 1997 © JOSSEY-BASS PUBLISHERS

Dogs and cats are easy. For one thing, by the time you get there, they'll be in the middle of a giant group head-pat and ear-scratch from an adoring audience. Birds are tougher. The old tennis coach in me would love to hit an overhead smash, but the audience would never tolerate such a dramatic solution. Birds require trickery and guile and lighting changes.

Wildlife-warning beeps usually come before school, at recess, or after school. So, when I heard that familiar sound the other day at 9:00 in the morning, I didn't think it would be animal-related. And I sure didn't expect it to be the type of animal it was.

"Beep—Mr. N., there's a raccoon on the playground." Now I'm no Daniel Boone or Davy Crockett, but having lived at least part of my life in the country, I know that a slow-moving, scared-of-nothing raccoon in broad daylight isn't something to be ignored. So, while my secretary Hilda called the police, my custodian Dave and I kept track of the varmint's movements and location.

Within a few minutes, a nice young police officer arrived; she was efficient and professional and took charge of tracking the beast. Shortly after that, the animal-control specialist pulled up. I was relieved that he neither looked nor acted like Ace Ventura. Certain that these two had things under control, Dave and I returned to the school and a more typical Friday morning.

Entering the office, I thought I'd be witty and sing the first few lines from the Beatles' song "Rocky Raccoon." (Yes, boomers, the White Album. For you youngsters—see, like, there used to be this, like, group called, like, the Beatles who were sorta like Paul McCartney's first, like, back-up group, and they, like, sang a song called "Rocky Raccoon.")

Several bars in, I realized that both Hilda and several young teachers were looking at me as if I were singing some Turkish folk song—in Turkish. And then it hit me. These "kids" had no idea how witty I was being. The White Album could have been a collection of Turkish folk songs for all they knew. This was not having the desired effect. I was being witty, and they were sure I'd finally gone 'round the bend.

Fortunately, one of my more mature (experienced? veteran? seasoned?) staff members walked in and said, " 'Rocky Raccoon.' The Beatles. White Album. Seventh track," and then explained to these "kids" what it was that I was doing.

Few things are more pitiful than wittiness that has to be explained. Later in the day, I got to thinking about what had happened. Maybe this was an early-warning sign from the gods of education that it was time for me to check out early retirement and the cost of a double-wide trailer in Florida. Maybe it was time to start singing "Here Comes the Sun." It's one thing to be "out of it" with the children in the school. Hey, nobody told me those stupid Power Rangers were identifiable by color. Who knew that "Foo Fighters" and "Blues Traveler" are bands and not some new laundry detergents?

But when your staff is more in tune with the Rollins Band than the Rolling Stones, what then? As a rookie teacher, I used to smile inwardly when one of the old-timers walked into the lounge whistling a big band classic. And now I'm the one making archaic musical references. As we used to say, Far out! What goes around really does come around.

I've decided not to worry about this. I'm not ready for some mobile home park for bewildered principals in Boca Raton. I can still handle the occasional hard day's night. I don't really want to stop the show. And I've got a few songs left to sing—just as in Sgt. Pepper.

Besides, I'll probably forget what happened in a couple of days anyway.

GORDON NUNEMAKER *is principal of Washington Elementary School in Sterling, Illinois.*

Faced with the challenges of high school leadership, the author finds stimulation and satisfaction in the people he works with and in the challenges themselves.

9

Relax and enjoy the show

Walter McClennen

WHEN I BEGAN my work as a high school principal, the superintendent who hired me took a balanced view of the world of educational administration. He said, "Just remember, we're in a movie, so relax, and enjoy the show." Remembering that observation has saved me as I have gone through the ups and downs of my first principalship. It reminds me that, although all decisions are important, I must be able to separate myself from the flow of events that can seem almost overwhelming. For every principal, the road gets rocky from time to time. In such times, the movie analogy has allowed me to keep things in a reasonable perspective: it has allowed me to have fun.

Marlborough High School has 1,140 students and a professional staff of ninety-five. We are a city and a suburb rolled into one in that we are located just forty-five minutes west of Boston and we feel the constant pressure of both housing and business development. During the two-and-one-half years that I have led the school, we have had our share of rocky times. I have worked under three superintendents. We have worked hard to emerge from probationary status that had been imposed on the school by our regional accrediting association. The school system witnessed a six-week "work to rule" job action, and we were just several days away

NEW DIRECTIONS FOR SCHOOL LEADERSHIP, NO. 5, FALL 1997 © JOSSEY-BASS PUBLISHERS

from a possible teachers' strike when a collective bargaining agreement was finally ratified. After five months as principal, the superintendent who hired me announced his resignation. Shall we say, it was not the easiest way to start out as a principal! I am reminded that when one signs on the dotted line, one never knows exactly how the job is going to develop.

Adding to our district challenges has been the seven-year educational reform program initiated by the Massachusetts Education Reform Act of 1993. On a weekly basis, some new mandate or implementation guideline arrives from the State Department of Education that requires immediate consultation with major stakeholders and then subsequent action.

Having had eighteen years of administrative experience as both a department head and assistant principal in two other systems, I felt confident and well prepared as I took on the task of school leadership in January of 1995. However, at times the challenges are daunting, and a reflection on the affirming and fulfilling aspects of the job is a welcome assignment. In spite of days that regularly start at 6:30 a.m. and frequently continue on to 9:00 or 10:00 p.m., the job is both a challenge and is—I can truthfully say—fun. The reasons for this are perhaps both known and unknown, but in the sections that follow, the reader will hopefully see why I enjoy such draining work.

Students

Take me to a good high school musical! In my current and previous schools, I have seen a number of shows and performances that match the quality and excitement of professional performances one can see in "the big city" thirty miles away. More than that, I know all the actors and actresses. I can congratulate them on Monday morning as they begin to wind down from the several months of preparation. My students have given me nights of basketball (or volleyball and soccer, and so on) that are as intense as professional and college competition. In almost all cases, these student athletes represent the school and the community in exemplary fashion. I am inspired by their intensity, their cooperation, and their desire to do well as much as by their success. Whereas the press may accentuate the negative and sensational, my contact with our students assures me that they are learning to take on full adult responsibilities. They are fun to work with, and for me and my staff, professional fulfillment starts with them.

I am constantly amazed at what teenagers can do! A new advisor recently took over the leadership of a dormant school newspaper. Very quickly, students got involved; they started to interview and they started to write. In eighteen short months, they have injected a new element into our school. There is news, opinion, and, needless to say, controversy. Each issue of *Panther Tracks* is now awaited eagerly by much of the school population. It has been a lively vehicle for school opinion, sharing, and debate. Students have seen what they can contribute to a school, and they have learned that they actually have some ownership of the institution.

Our peer intervention teams hosted the AIDS quilt and its "Names Project." A dedicated group of young people assisted by staff and community leaders spent a year in the application process, in preparation, and in helping out several local families who had lost loved ones and wished to contribute a panel for the quilt. It was both a proud and somber moment in Marlborough High School when these young folks opened up our field house for three days of public viewing of the eight massive quilts on Thanksgiving weekend of last year. Both students and the community at large benefited from this major undertaking. As principal, a real sense of the great value of educators' work permeated my being during the week leading up to this event. Students were becoming invested in assisting the community at large. They also were growing as individuals who could understand and respond to the needs of others.

Every increment of growth and maturity that we facilitate in our daily work contributes to three futures: each student's, our local community's, and the nation's. As principal, I get to see and contribute to this growth and I can play a key role in helping and encouraging teachers to make their contributions. Understandably the most challenging part of this work is with disciplinary incidents. A student is sassy or disrespectful toward a teacher. Mouse balls disappear from the computer lab. Unwanted banners appear high up on the field-house roof. Signs of alcohol creep into school functions. Sometimes students have even become assaultive or have said or done things that are classified as sexual harassment.

My challenge is to remember that the vast majority of our students are not causing these problems and to see that good comes from the bad decisions that kids sometimes make. Discussions take place; parents are involved; sometimes law enforcement authorities must be included. Counselors and social service providers are engaged in problem resolution. Time and energy are expended by staff sometimes to the point of exhaustion, but our students learn, grow, and mature.

School principals are a central part of this process; the messages we convey with our actions give a clear sense of direction for all staff and the community. As we go about our business with "out-of-line" students, I am delighted to see them mature and move toward the excitement and celebration of senior year and graduation. As education critics focus on the supposed failures of schools, they would do well to look more closely at the broad and pervasive successes we have as we work with our students. As principals, this is what we do, and our yearly observation of student success and growth keeps us going!

Teachers

The most important task I have in terms of the district and its long-term success is the hiring of new personnel. This past year, I had the opportunity to hire fourteen new teachers. It was a very busy spring and summer, but a superb chance to bring in some young, exciting, and talented teachers who could spark student interest in learning and to attain greater minority representation on our staff so it would better mirror the diverse student population we serve. I worked closely with my department heads to review all résumés and supporting materials. I was overwhelmed and encouraged to see what excellent backgrounds and skills some young people are bringing with them as they enter the teaching field. We hired two excellent subject area teachers who are fluent in Spanish. This has helped our school considerably as we try to meet the varied needs of our growing Hispanic population. Most of our new teachers brought educational technology skills that have proven helpful to both our students and our more seasoned staff. Bringing exciting and talented (both younger and older!) staff on board has raised the level of energy and purpose for students, staff, and me. My only disappointment has been my inability to significantly increase the minority representation on my staff. However, principals thrive on challenge, and I intend to keep working on this goal and ultimately to achieve success.

The other role I enjoy playing is that of teacher support person or listener. Teachers come into my office at 6:45 in the morning to seek advice on how to work with a certain difficult student. Or sometimes the issue will be a parent who is angry or who does not seem to understand what the teacher is trying to do to aid his or her child. Sometimes the issue is related to a conflict (or potential conflict) with another staff member. Although the issues are challenging and sometimes defy resolution, these "people problems" do have reasonable paths to resolution, if we have the time, common sense, and patience to commit to them. As I listen to my teachers and discuss such issues with them, I usually feel invigorated and confirmed by the progress that we make.

These types of concerns can erode staff energy, time, and possibly commitment. When I honor them, staff typically express appreciation for the time, consideration, and sharing of perspectives that I have invested. I have learned to be sure that sufficient time is given to any staff member who is seeking my advice. If I offer the time and a sympathetic ear, I can indeed serve in one of my most valued capacities—facilitator of teacher success.

Parents and Community

We can all recall difficult disagreements we have had with our parent constituents. But I prefer to remember the more numerous parents who have thanked teachers, coaches, and me for assisting with the educational and social growth of their children. Whether it was the improved format for the annual fall open house, the great success of the music or drama program, the added advanced placement courses, or increased access to computer technology, parents are constantly saying "thank you." These kind words of thanks make each day more enjoyable. They help to recharge the batteries and get both me and others ready for the challenges of the next day.

I am particularly appreciative of the lightning bolt ideas parents can have that help immeasurably to improve our school. "Let's have a big banner that says *This is Panther Country* hanging at the front entry. I think I can get support from the fire department and some local businesses." "Would you like to have us bring in a table full of food for Teacher Appreciation Week?" "Have you seen this article on diversity training for schools? Maybe you could utilize some of the ideas." "Teacher *X* has really helped my daughter, and I'm going to write you a letter to that effect." "We have a committee of parents and community members who will be putting together the annual all-nighter-after-prom party. Could you just be sure to get a message about not driving and drinking in the May newsletter and encourage staff participation? We'll do the rest!!" Over and over, it is most gratifying to have parents in my school combine with active community members to help our students.

On the other side, we know there will be days of conflict. From time to time, parents and principals disagree on the wisdom of a certain course of action. However, I have found that, if I am consistent and if I am true to fundamental beliefs about what it is that a student and a school community need, the wisdom and value of the course taken will come to be recognized. This past spring, our school confronted what I call the "principal's nightmare." Close to a quarter of the senior class got involved in a prank "decorating" the school that got totally out of hand. Demeaning graffiti, along with the defacing and malicious destruction of school property, led to several weeks of administrative and police investigation. Graduation activities were modified as disciplinary action was taken against a large number of students.

As can often be the case in such disciplinary matters, many parents were not in agreement with the administration's position. After a month of meetings with parents and students, the dust began to settle and I could look back at this particular "movie script" with a more balanced view than when I was in the midst of the boiling cauldron. By holding the line and explaining the basis for my actions while, at the same time, taking the time to listen to parents, the school ended up getting through the crisis and having a superb graduation for the senior class. It was a most gratifying moment for me. I am certain we will grow from the events of the spring and become a better place in future years.

Forming a close working relationship with parent and community groups, although difficult to do, is important and affirming work. Our school council, a major element of the Education Reform Act of 1993, has significantly contributed to making our school a better place for students. Fifteen times a year, the sixteen members of the council meet for two to three hours in the conference room beside my office. Three student members, five teachers, six parents, and a community member serve in an advisory capacity to me. The council's tasks are basically to review the needs of the school and produce a school improvement plan in order to address those needs. They also review the school budget and the Time and Learning Plan for the school that is required under the Education Reform of Act of 1993.

I always leave the council's evening meetings feeling exhilarated. When I arrived at MHS, many questioned the school's ability to offer the level of education that the community expected. The press often portrayed the school and the school system in a negative light. The council rose to the occasion and worked hard to ensure that the accrediting agency's concerns were addressed and that the new administration of the school would leave no stone unturned in its efforts to make Marlborough High an exemplary school. I have strived to make our discussions open and frank. They have always been lively! I have been pleased that neither the students nor the parents have at any time felt bashful about speaking their minds and we are a stronger school for it.

One of our recurrent discussions is around Scholastic Aptitude Tests and the concern of some parents that a school goal should be the raising of our average SAT scores. Some council members see this test data as a good measure of our success; others see these (and other tests) as far too restrictive in terms of the total educational mission that we have before us. We have had heated discussions. Despite the fireworks this sometimes generates, much good emerges as it has focused us on the key question of student outcomes. As we implement our next three-year plan, we will be forced to resolve this fundamental issue of how we will know if we are (or are not) doing a good job. Maybe SAT results will be part of the mix, maybe not. Whatever the case, the decision will be made by representatives of the key stakeholders in the school, and that is the way it should be.

The role that student members of the council have played in this predominantly adult forum has been very rewarding for me. As we discussed the pros and cons of moving into block scheduling, the most valuable viewpoints were those of students who, on a daily basis, lived through the classes of our trial-run year. It was clear to them that some teachers were working very hard to experiment with the new eighty-five minute class periods and that others were not as invested. Perhaps it was the lack of sufficient training or perhaps it was the rapidity of the change, but it was the quality of the students' observations that suggested that caution was the better path as we experimented with this currently popular restructuring innovation. As we debated this innovation, the response of both parent and faculty council members made it clear to the students that they were coequal members. The more we adults can bring high school students into the decision-making process, the better off we will be. I am proud to see this happening at our school.

Change

Of all the things that keep me going as a principal, my role as change agent sits at the top of the list. In Massachusetts in the last several years, our Education Reform Act has put a real societal focus on the need to improve schools. Although society and the law have not yet given the principal all the tools necessary to effect all the changes that should take place, there is a growing recognition that principals need sufficient autonomy to lead their schools if improvements are to really take hold.

The parts I have played in helping our school to change have been numerous. Most important, our reform law has given me and other Massachusetts principals more autonomy in hiring, nonrenewal of contracts, and dismissal decisions. This increased authority should permit principals to shape their staffs into the high-performing professional forces so essential to student learning. At Marlborough High, we are generating a deeper understanding of interdisciplinary instruction. An American Studies course, team-taught by teachers from the social studies and the English departments, weaves together American history and American literature, permitting students to see how American literature and the evolving social and political contexts are related.

We are beginning to collaborate to make learning more relevant to students' lives. A tech-prep program has affected staff positively as teachers of math, science, English, and business, along with guidance counselors, prepare students to be more forward-thinking as they consider how their education is connected to the world of work. These staff members meet weekly to coordinate this innovative program. Students who once wondered, How does this relate to real life? are beginning to see direct relationships between school and adult career realities due to such cooperative teacher initiatives.

We are becoming more closely linked both with neighboring businesses and schools and with distant schools. The business community has become a vital partner to the school system as both volunteer time and money have hooked us to the Internet. A federal technology grant to neighboring Hudson has brought five area high schools together as we explore how our Internet capability can link fifty schools nationally and internationally in what will be known as the Virtual High School. Our students have excitedly joined in our staff's effort to enter the electronically connected world. To confront the numerous questions that arise out of such a project, five area high school principals meet on a regular basis in a way that hasn't happened before. These developments have made my work more fulfilling and our teachers' work less isolated.

Increased student intervention in school community issues has also been an encouraging new direction. At Marlborough High, a very active peer intervention team runs a variety of programs that are all founded on the concept that the students themselves are the best vehicles for bringing about student (and consequently social) change. These students meet monthly for focused evening meetings on issues such as violence prevention, harassment, and substance abuse. On a daily and weekly basis, they carry their positive social message through the school by both words and deeds.

As we respond to society's demand for significant change in our schools, we are called on as principals to extend beyond our more traditional role of "keeper of order" or "manager." I am challenged and excited by the call for us to lead and to become key players in social and community progress. These challenges and the risks they carry with them as we seek to make a real difference in community life make our work deeply meaningful.

The job of principal may not be easy, but for me it revolves daily around making a difference for students, adults, and the community. We constantly interact with a fascinating variety of people. We have the opportunity to contribute to their learning in ways we could not likely do in most other professions. I have found that if I approach my job in the right perspective, I find many reasons to enjoy it and feel rewarded by it. The script of the movie will be different in every case and we will never control that script as much as we might like. Nevertheless, the role of principal is one that offers us professional fulfillment, the pride of significant accomplishments, and the enjoyment of working and growing with people of all ages.

WALTER MCCLENNEN *is principal of Marlborough High School, Marlborough, Massachusetts.*

The author describes how, as principal of a rural elementary
school, he is constantly refueled by his contact with children.

10

Hardly a week goes by

Jack Pickens

IF THERE IS one thing I have come to accept in my role as a school
principal, it is that someone will always remind me that I have an
arduous job. Hardly a week goes by without a parent, staff member, or community member commenting, "How do you do this?
I'm glad you do this and not me!" or "What a thankless job!" or "I
guess that's why you get the big bucks." Indeed, we principals face
more than our share of confrontational situations, punitive actions,
and insanely bureaucratic paperwork. Our work can test our verve
if not our amity. What many people fail to consider is the bigger
picture of the principal as facilitator, inspirational leader, and
change agent.

As I consider why I come to work every morning and I mull over
the many hats I wear as principal, I find myself returning to the
very first hat I wore as an educator: the teacher hat. The twenty-
three years I spent in K–8 classrooms prepared me for the next
twelve in administration by clarifying my priorities. I enjoy what I
do simply because I am able as a principal to live the vision I had
when I entered education. That vision depicted a principal who was
the leader of a model school, a school that was continually evolving and striving for excellence. A principal who sincerely cared
about all members of the school community and who was engaged

NEW DIRECTIONS FOR SCHOOL LEADERSHIP, NO. 5, FALL 1997 © JOSSEY-BASS PUBLISHERS

in their learning. I envisioned a staff of eager life-long learners who candidly shared their values, thoughts, and ideas in a safe, professional setting.

This vision resulted, in part, from my frustrations as a classroom teacher, from a desire to fulfill the more fundamental vision of a learner-centered school I had developed as a teacher. I knew that although many teachers and I had the energy, ideas, and willingness to make education better for children, the task was nearly impossible unless the site administrator's actions supported change and fostered a team approach. The vision I had of a school administrator did not place the principal above, but alongside. As a principal I wanted to be sure that all new ideas were thoroughly and respectfully considered and when adopted were supported by the staff and the administration.

Guiding and teaching

Over the course of my twelve years as principal, I have come to appreciate the many rewards that this position offers me. I cherish the opportunity to function as a compassionate, nurturing, and caring mentor who celebrates the success of each individual and the school community at large. I embrace the daily opportunities to help teachers fulfill their visions as educators. I make it my primary task to support the ideas of others, give them suggestions, encourage and pick them up when they fall down, and celebrate their successes. Where else outside the classroom can one find so many nurturing tasks to fill the day?

My happiest and most meaningful days are when a teacher comes to me with an idea that she or he has and I can take an active role in making it a reality. Recently our entire primary staff grew concerned with the success of our reading program. Boiling with ideas, they came to me to share their challenge. It was exciting for me to be a part of this high-energy brainstorming; I felt privileged to be associated with such highly motivated and professional folks. Needless to say, the plan that emerged for an early intervention program called for sacrifices in every area and was not without some budgetary constraints. My role was to sort out the web of ideas, find ways to hurdle the obstacles, and eventually facilitate the implementation.

There were times in the process when the project seemed too fraught with obstacles to ever become a reality. My pleasure came not only from helping to find ways to surmount those obstacles but also from keeping my dedicated colleagues from caving in to the frustration. Today we have the beginnings of what I hope one day will be a complete early reading intervention program. In analyzing the process, I see my role as that of a guide who nudged a bit here, pulled when needed, and always kept the vision in view by clarifying, redefining, and untangling.

Is this not really the definition of a teacher? As a principal, I have the opportunity to practice what I preach. I see it as my job to model the behaviors that define a good teacher. I guide my colleagues to new horizons while learning alongside them. Therein lies the real reason I pursue my vision: I can continue to serve as a teacher. My influence, although not as large a factor on any one individual, multiplies each teacher's work and becomes a larger factor in the school as a whole.

I enjoy the feeling I get when, as a staff, we come together with all our energy to rethink, rework, and retool to make a program work. One of the more rewarding examples of this is the process we used in applying for California Distinguished School Status in 1995. With a determination to examine what we were all about, we completed the application process and, along the way, developed a new understanding of ourselves and the institution we are charged with running.

The ultimate reward from this process was one shared by all of us. When we received recognition from the state, our confidence in ourselves was doubly recharged. Since then I recognize how this award really manifested itself in a renewed energy to become even better. We knew we were doing a good job, but as educators all of us were aware of the cloud of the constant criticism public education receives. This ever-present cloud unwittingly cast a shadow of doubt over us, making us reluctant to apply for this recognition. I felt that, like many students I have taught, our staff needed to pursue their dream with a burst of inner resolve and confidence. My part in this process was again that of the guide who encourages and facilitates.

I needed to share my belief that we were well on our way to being an excellent school and to pull along the others to make us one. The Distinguished School Principal plaque that hangs on my office wall is a constant reminder of what our staff can do and of my responsibility to enable them to do what they do best: teach children. I marvel at how our willing staff can take an idea and make it into a practical and working program. Believing, as Francis Keppel did, that education is too important to be left solely in the hands of educators, our staff developed yearly Student Conference days. Resource people from across Northern California come to our little mountain school and present workshops centered on a curriculum area. How fulfilling it is to see children choosing which workshops they will attend, see them interact with visiting professionals, watch the professionals make acquaintance with each other, and watch parents and community members sitting in on workshops with obvious interest. Every participant is learning right before my eyes! Sitting in a reading circle discussing Boyer's *The Basic School* (1995) not only offers intellectual stimulation but demonstrates that when dedicated individuals come together to learn, all things are possible.

Be a public learner

A plaque hangs above my office door that says simply, *Jack Pickens, Head Learner*. It is often a topic of conversation when visitors notice it for the first time and wonder what it means. The title was given to me by the teachers shortly after I assumed the position as the West Point Elementary School Principal. The title is one that I am extremely proud to carry and is emblematic of my greatest accomplishment. It says that I am a learner who learns each and every day.

I feel that it also states that I do not know all there is to know about education and that I am willing and eager to hear what others have to say.

A community member recently remarked that I am good for the staff because I serve as a father figure. That one interests me. I have never considered myself a father figure for the staff. As I think about this, however, the role begins to fit rather comfortably. I do enjoy the respect that comes when I can help the staff reach consensus, when they feel comfortable enough to share their professional and personal problems, and when they solicit my input. I think that one of the staff's greatest expectations of me is that I will listen—not only to the tales of classroom success and failure but also to personal and professional needs.

A second expectation is that I will compromise and change my mind if presented with evidence that the alternative is better for children. I enjoy being seen as one who seeks out new knowledge and is continually learning and as one who makes decisions fairly, equitably, and inclusively without the overlay of politics. Perhaps equally rewarding is the opportunity to help parents as they try to sort out their lives. I am often asked for advice or direction by parents. Where can they get help collecting child support? What alternative program is there for their son who dropped out? How do you access a women's shelter or mental health services? So, like a father, I can be counted on to listen, guide, and assist when asked. So perhaps I am the father figure to some people. If I can help in that role, then I accept it.

And then there are the daily contacts with the students who come to my office to exhibit their newly found reading skills, to receive their birthday cards (and endure the Head Learner's dramatic if somewhat off-key rendition of *Happy Birthday to You*), to proudly announce that they were sent to receive the Good Apple Award, to read a diagnostic passage, to bring me a sample of their latest cooking adventure, or simply to tell me that things are better and that they are having a great day. Listening to first-grade students read with great pride in their accomplishment never fails to bring a smile to my face nor to remind me of the love I have for what we do as educators. I need no more reward from my job than to hear an emergent reader show his or her skill!

Each month we have a Good Apple luncheon for the month's Good Apples. These are at-risk students who exhibit great coping skills by simply coming to school each day. Many of them come from home situations that offer little more than a roof over their heads. The pride they exhibit in receiving their pins and joining me for lunch consummates my work. Recognizing these children as models of what one can do when one puts a shoulder to the wheel is without a doubt a reward I share with them.

Enjoying the small things

I cannot close this chapter without noting some of the seemingly small things that sustain me in my work. If you were to ask one group of fifth graders why I come to work, they might say it is to play four-square. I delight in the constant invitations to join them in a quick game (which often ends up being the entire lunch recess period). The students enjoy it when one of them gets the principal out (which, I am afraid, is becoming a more frequent occurrence).

Other students might say I come to school to sit next to them during lessons so that I can check up on them. There is no better way to know what is going on in a school than to sit and work alongside students. For a few moments, I am participating in learning and teaching as our children do. I am with our students in a way that helps them know me as a learner and as a teacher.

I enjoy my role as greeter, saying good morning to parents as they drop their children off at the curb each day. It amazes me how this gesture creates goodwill and confidence in the school. I cannot count the times that parents have expressed their appreciation for this simple use of fifteen minutes. It starts my day on a bright note as I hope it does for the students and parents.

And so it goes, year after year, day after day, child after child. My principalship is an adventure in serving, nurturing, and smiling. I am sustained by always remembering that the business of a leader is to turn hurdles into opportunities and failures into successes. Without a firm understanding of myself and my limits, the job could easily consume me. I try to keep in mind that, although my job is tremendously important, I do not work in an emergency ward. Things will get done and solutions will be found, but only if all of us go about our business with calmness, confidence, and conviction.

When times get tense, I remember that in this world of rapid change, one thing remains: learning. All of us are learning each and every day. And if that does not work I take a walk around the school gardens. Hardly a week goes by . . .

Reference

Boyer, Ernest. *The Basic School: A Community for Learning.* Princeton, N.J.: Carnegie Foundation for the Advancement of Teaching, 1995.

JACK PICKENS *is principal of West Point Elementary School, West Point, California.*

Index